PIZZAZZ
FOR PENNIES

Designer Clothes
for Children

Other books in the *Creative Machine Arts* series,
available from Chilton:

The Complete Book of Machine Embroidery
by Robbie and Tony Fanning

The Expectant Mother's Wardrobe Planner
by Rebecca Dumlao

PIZZAZZ
FOR PENNIES

Designer Clothes
for Children

BARB FORMAN

CHILTON BOOK COMPANY Radnor, Pennsylvania

Copyright © 1986 by Barb Forman
All Rights Reserved
Published in Radnor, Pennsylvania 19089, by Chilton Book Company

Photographs by Bill Scherer, except where otherwise noted
Wooden goose peg rack by John Gilbert, Country Woods
Acrylic cardigan and crewneck sweaters by Bluebird Knitwear
Book design by William E. Lickfield
Manufactured in the United States of America

Library of Congress Cataloging-in-Publication Data
Forman, Barb.
Pizzazz for pennies.
(Creative machine arts series)
Includes index.
I. Children's clothing. I. Title. II. Series.
TT635.F68   1986   746.9'2   86-47610
ISBN 0-8019-7729-0

2 3 4 5 6 7 8 9 0   5 4 3 2 1 0 9 8 7

To
JONATHON AND JAMIE,
my inspirations, and
to my mom
NATALIE GRIFFIN
with all my love

Contents

Foreword

A pleasure of being with children is that they help you see common objects with fresh eyes. We always picked dandelions and blew away the fuzz with our daughter, saying "Make a wish! Make a wish!" One day when she was three, the wind lofted dandelion fuzz through the air. Our daughter was enchanted. "Oh, look," she exclaimed. "Wishes!"

I immediately appliquéd a dandelion head to a plain jumper I had made, representing the fuzz by radiating lines of satin stitch. She loved it and I loved it but, truthfully, it didn't look much like a dandelion.

I'm not a designer, so each appliqué on the tons of kids' clothes I decorated was a struggle. I used the designs from coloring books a lot, but I still made mistakes. That's why I wish I'd had Barb Forman's book when I was a young mother.

First of all, Barb's designs are show-stoppers, especially with the extra three-dimensional touches using buttons, bows, and other trims. But, more importantly, she would have saved me time and money — time, because she's worked out all the kinks of each design, while I spent most of my time unkinking; and money, because I could have made up her designs as gifts, instead of rushing around at the last minute spending too much on presents for playmates.

I especially like Barb's idea of transforming inexpensive or used clothing, like a $3 sweatshirt, into something special by adding an appliqué. Why didn't I think of that? For some reason, I had tunnel vision and always made a new outfit to decorate. How silly! I could have had a finished garment in one night instead of four.

Barb has other good ideas — other ways to use her designs, adaptations for boys' clothing, quick gift-giving, ideas for making things with pizzazz in one hour, and much more.

Her book is one of three in our new series, Creative Machine Arts. These books, written by the best authors, cover the most up-to-date topics in the field of fashion and creative uses of the sewing machine.

I always loved decorating children's clothing, no matter how pathetic my dandelions, and was mildly sad when our daughter grew too old. But happily, all around me is a mini-baby boom. Friends are having first babies and fourth babies and afterthought babies. Good! Now I have an excuse to sew Barb Forman outfits for those children. Lucky me, lucky you, lucky kids.

Robbie Fanning

Series Editor and author,
The Complete Book of Machine Embroidery

Preface

When motherhood smiled down on me, she had an extra twinkle in her eye. I was soon the mother of two little darlings—just 10½ months apart. Wanting to dress my tots in only the finest apparel, I soon found it was beyond my financial means. Faced with champagne tastes and beer pockets, I longingly admired the array of lovely attire, able to choose only one outfit per child from the most exclusive shops in town.

Determination became my motto. I could teach myself to sew and *make* those wonderful clothes. I became the Sherlock Holmes of the kids' circuit, studying intently what made the clothes so very special. Some of my happiest days were spent window shopping at the expensive children's boutiques on Michigan Avenue in Chicago. After memorizing my favorite outfits, I raced to the women's room and sketched them, making copious notes on all their special details. After days of research, several things became clear. The allure of the tiny finery could be broken down into three basic rules: classic lines; bright, clear colors; and simple yet catchy appliqués with a crisp look.

Armed with a $66 sewing machine that could only straight and zigzag stitch, I bought a simple pattern for an A-line jumper and overalls. Within a month, I had worked out the kinks and was making clothes that I was proud to have my children wear. The clothing looked like a million dollars, yet had been made for just a fraction of retail cost.

While my toddlers napped in the afternoons, I sewed to my heart's content. People began stopping us on the street to ask where I had purchased such delightful duds for my children. I smiled while the kids chirped, "Mommy made them!" In addition to saving money and knowing that my children were well-dressed, there was a wonderful sense of accomplishment.

If I can do it, so can you.

This book is organized by seasons, so you can start at any time. Your scrap basket will yield delightful trims, buttons, and special touches to bring a smile. Study commercial patterns available and choose one or two basic patterns that include the following: jumper, shorts, pants, shortall, overall, and a simple jacket. With these basics and a few purchased staples, your child's wardrobe is ready to bloom. Happy sewing!

A number of people offered their help and support in the preparation of this book. My heart-felt thanks to Margaret Dittman for her guidance; to Joyce Gillis, a friend who always listened; to Kathleen Shaw for her invaluable counsel; to Penny Quint for the laughter, advice, and endless hours of help; and to Robbie Fanning, who made my dream a reality.

CHAPTER 1

An Insider's Guide to
Pizzazz for Pennies

There is nothing to equal the marvelous feeling I get entering an exclusive children's boutique. The bright, crisp colors coupled with their whimsical accents always make me smile. What makes these clothes so very special? Why does a simple appliquéd jumper have a price tag of $50 + or a jacket $65 +? The answer almost seems too easy: classic style, excellent quality fabrics, and machine appliqué.

Quality children's wear carried in select boutiques and carriage trade shops can be duplicated easily. Study the window displays of stores or "shop" the pages of high-quality mail-order catalogs. What makes the garment special? The styles are most often classic jumpers and shortalls in bright, clear colors, accented with appliqué. Make note of special ribbons, buttons, or novel trims. Is the garment monogrammed or personalized? By breaking the garment into categories of style, color, appliqué, and trim, you can then see how simply the pieces make the whole.

One of my favorite projects is to take an inexpensive item and dress it up. You can start simply with a pair of kneesocks. Sew decorative buttons up the outside of the legs and top with a bright bow: *instant pizzazz.* A pair of white nylon kneesocks can be stenciled, using one or two colors to match a spring ensemble. The result is the equivalent of $6 socks shown in popular mail-order catalogs.

To understand how to break down the design elements of a designer garment, let's use as an example the Beach Bear Sweatshirt for a girl shown in Chapter 3. Begin with a purchased sweatshirt (watch for sales and the savings can be significant). The lavender sweatshirt used was on sale for $3.99. Study the various parts that make up the item:

1. Sleeves: length was cut to short style, edged with eyelet and elastic casing. Bright bow trim was added. The left sleeve is appliquéd with a smiling sun face and touch of embroidery.

2. Main appliqué: Teddy bear appliqué is done with pastel colors in simple shapes. Bow and flowers add 3-D charm.

3. Bow at right side of neckline balances the design.

The end result is a charming beach cover-up that would retail for $35.00.

Repeat this exercise with clothing you see while shopping or browsing through catalogs. Ask yourself what makes the item special and make notes if that helps you. Watch for special trims, ribbons, or buttons. Those bits and pieces can take an item from simple to snazzy. You can see the transformation in Figs. 1-1 through 1-4, showing the boy's version of the sweatshirt as each segment is added, taking it from plain to pizzazz.

This book features:

1. Projects that incorporate purchased items that you embellish;
2. Appliqué designs to add to a garment you sew from a pattern;
3. Complete patterns for small projects and accessories.

Each season of the year has a special theme, along with additional variations. Approximate costs are included as guidelines.

Bright solid colors are used, along with small prints and pin dots. Poplin, Trigger and corduroys are ideal fabrics because of their durability and versatility.

Once you have begun sewing for your favorite youngster, the savings will be overshadowed by the creative joy you experience. Use this book as a jumping-off point. Choose your own theme for a season. Sports, toys, gardening, airplanes, or model cars might hold a special appeal for your child. Simple drawings are easily transposed to appliqué. Coloring books are wonderful sources for easy-to-use ideas. The possibilities are limitless.

Before you begin any of the projects, please review the following general how-to information section. It will give you a basic understanding of the techniques used, and explain materials needed. Please also read the complete instructions for each design project before cutting into fabrics, as there may be exceptions to these general instructions.

SUPPLIES AND TOOLS

The supplies and tools listed are suggestions to guide you in making the clothing shown in this book. The materials listed are the materials that were used to create the project as photographed. Always feel free to use what works best for you and to use the supplies, tools, and materials list as guidelines — not absolute requirements. The most helpful suggestion that I can give you is to use what you have on hand and *improvise*: it can result in wonderful clothing you will be proud to say you created yourself.

Scissors

Scissors are one of the most important tools that a sewer has. Keep two pairs on hand: one for paper and one for fabrics. My special pair of sewing scissors has a red ribbon tied in a bow on the handle to alert me to use them only for fabric.

Embroidery scissors are also ideal for cutting small shapes, snipping curves and corners, and cutting into hard-to-reach areas.

Fig. 1–1 Cutting out the appliqué pieces. "From Plain to Pizzazz" sequence photos by Marnie Leonard.

Fig. 1–2 The completed sun appliqué in position.

Fig. 1–3 Teddy appliqué
pieces pinned in place.

Fig. 1–4 Presto! The com-
pleted sweatshirt.

4

Pins and Needles

One of the best purchases that I made this year was a magnetic pin cushion. It's ideal as a paperweight or pin cushion, and also holds my seam ripper, embroidery scissors, and tiny safety pins.

Extra-long quilting pins are a great help when working on multilayered projects. An assortment of hand and sewing machine needles is a good investment: you can determine your favorite size, but will probably use them all for one project or another. Crewel needles are handy for embroidered touches.

When doing machine appliqué, be sure your needles are sharp and the correct size for the fabric you are working with, so as not to overstress and pull the fabrics. I most often use a size 12(80) for machine appliqué, especially for fabrics such as Trigger or sailcloth. When sewing any projects using knits, be sure to use a ballpoint sewing machine needle for best results.

Threads

When sewing clothes for children, sturdy construction is a must. Use poly/cotton thread for main construction and extra-fine 100% cotton thread for machine appliqué stitches. If you find good quality white or off-white thread on sale, buy several spools. It is excellent for a standard bobbin thread when doing machine appliqué. After a long process of trial-and-error, I am especially fond of the quality of Metrosene thread, but, once again, use the brand that works best for you on *your* machine.

Fabrics

When yardages are given in a materials list, I have assumed that the fabric is at least 44″ wide. Pre-wash all fabrics as soon as you get home from the store so that you are always ready to begin a project at a moment's notice.

Try to use fabrics of common fiber content: this will prevent one fabric from shrinking or colors from running, which can ruin the appliqué and the outfit. If your main fabric choice is poly/cotton, use appliqué pieces in poly/cotton or cotton. I prefer to back all pieces to be appliquéd with lightweight iron-on interfacing. It is easiest to fuse the interfacing to the back of fabric pieces first, and then cut out the appliqué. Most fabric shops will have lightweight interfacing available in packages of three yards for a very reasonable price. Two three-yard packages will make all of the projects in this book. The interfacing stabilizes the fabrics so they do not pucker or fray — yet does not make the appliqué too bulky. This is especially important when appliquéing more than one layer.

When felt is listed in the materials list for a project, use only acrylic felt. Wool-blend felts shrink, so you cannot launder them. Acrylic felt launders well — ask at fabric shops about fiber content and purchase only felt with 100% acrylic fiber for appliqué to children's clothes. The felt I used for the projects in this book is from The Felters Co. (see Sources of Supply).

5

When batting or fleece is called for in the materials list for a project, I prefer to use Thermolam Plus batting. Thermolam Plus is a lofty needle-punched fleece that adds warmth without bulk—especially nice for children's wear. This batting will not beard when you quilt—another plus. If you have a batting that works well for you, by all means use it; otherwise, I recommend the Thermolam.

Glues

With the advent of good nonsoluble glues on the market, a lot of busy work can be cut down. Thoroughly read all information on the glue containers to be sure it will work for the project you are making. Hot glue guns and glue sticks are excellent for accessory items.

Pens, Pencils, and Paints

Have on hand a few soft #2 pencils and a package of good quality white tissue paper, which is available in stationery or discount stores. These are needed for tracing patterns. Water-soluble marking pens make detail embroidery work and topstitching a snap. Using the pattern as an example, you can draw in the features shown, embroider or paint them, and have the markings dissolve automatically. I prefer the pen whose ink evaporates within 48 hours or can be erased by dampening with water.

If you dislike embroidery work (stitch details are provided on page 26), hand-paint detail using acrylic paints. For children's clothing that is frequently laundered, allow paints to dry 24 hours and permanently set paints by using a pressing cloth and steam iron set on "cotton" to iron over the painted area.

℞ for Care

CAUTION: Avoid the use of buttons, bells, pompoms, and other "munchables" if the garments are for a child aged three or under. Toddlers usually inspect their clothing with small curious hands, so secure any trims with extra care.

SHOPPING HINTS

The very best advice that I can offer is to watch for sales! Look for discounts on notions and stock up on threads, bias tape, ribbon, and buttons. Write approximate yardages needed for basics like pants, jumpers, and jackets, on an index card and tuck it in your wallet. When you come across a good reduction on mini-dot prints, poplin solids, gingham, Trigger, or other favorite staples, you'll be prepared to stock up on a rainbow assortment of colors in the correct amounts. Because children's wear requires such minimal yardage, check the remnant tables for bargains, too. Scraps of fabrics you might already have from other projects are ideal for trims, facings, or appliqués.

End-of-season sales on sweaters, solid-color sweatsuits, and accessories can

6

be substantial. When you have a favorite brand of sweater or jacket, guess approximate size needs for the upcoming year and stock up when you see the items reduced at the season's end.

Chain discount stores are a wonderful source of clothing to which you can add special embellishments. Packages containing three pairs of nylon or cableknit kneesocks can be purchased for the price of one pair at a fancy boutique, then trimmed for that special custom touch. Dime stores will offer a treasure trove of delights, such as ribbon bundle specials and assortments of charms and buttons at a discounted price.

Women's specialty stores and avant garde stationery stores sometimes carry an extraordinary line of imported ribbons and buttons. When I find a special ribbon that I can't live without, my rule of thumb is to buy two yards: enough for pigtails and to spur my imagination at a later date.

APPLIQUÉ AND QUILTING TECHNIQUES

Don't underestimate the importance of making careful and accurate patterns. Most of the patterns in this book are full-size, ready for you to trace. When you begin a project, check the pattern and directions for seam allowances. Always include all lines, placement details, and labeling when you trace the patterns from this book. This will save you time and headaches later.

Machine appliqué designs are cut on pattern outlines, without seam or hem allowance. If you plan to hand appliqué, add 1/4" seam allowance around the perimeter of each appliqué piece before cutting. For greater durability, patterns that will be used several times can be glued to lightweight cardboard or plastic before they are cut out.

Another alternative to tracing patterns is to photocopy them. Check first to be sure that the reproduction is accurate. If you need designs reduced or enlarged to fit the size you are making, a photocopy shop can help you for a reasonable charge. Keep in mind the copyright laws: patterns are for personal sewing use only!

Appliqué consists of shapes cut from one piece of fabric and applied to another. The shapes, sizes, and colors you choose become the appliqué "picture."

Traditionally, appliqué was stitched by hand, but machine appliqué is recommended for children's clothes because of its durability. It withstands a great deal of wear and tear.

Appliqué techniques are the same whether you are making a garment or enhancing a purchased one. However, if you are making the garment, it is easier to appliqué individual pieces before assembling the garment.

After you have chosen the project, traced or copied the pattern, and selected your fabrics, back all fabrics to be used for the appliqué with lightweight iron-on interfacing. I always use a piece of tissue paper between the interfacing and my iron: the fusing material can sometimes melt through, causing a sticky residue on your iron. The tissue paper barrier is the perfect solution, allowing you to see through to the areas you are fusing.

Position and pin pieces according to pattern placement guides. I only use fusible webbing under tricky or small appliqué pieces. Use the technique that works best for you.

Machine Appliqué

The satin stitch used for appliqué can be sewn by any zigzag sewing machine. It is the zigzag stitch, with stitches placed so closely together that they form a thick solid line, that outlines each appliqué piece, with approximately 20 stitches per inch.

If machine appliqué is new to you, there are a few quick, and easy ways to master this technique. Start by cutting hearts and stars from felt and appliquéing them to a closely woven practice fabric, such as poplin or Trigger. Because felt does not fray, it is a good starter fabric. The curves, points, and straight lines of these shapes will give you the variety needed to master appliquéing any shape. Practice pivoting at corners and curves until you are satisfied with the results. Your lines may wiggle a little at first, but with practice, you will improve quickly.

Next, practice appliquéing hearts and stars cut out of mini-dot, solid, or calico scraps you have on hand. Once again, be sure to back these pieces with lightweight iron-on interfacing for a better finished look.

Slightly loosen the upper tension of your sewing machine until you can see the upper thread on the underside of your sample appliqué scrap. This way, the bobbin thread will always be hidden so you won't need to constantly change bobbins when you change upper thread color to match the appliqué piece.

It also helps to use an embroidery appliqué presser foot. This foot is scooped out underneath, allowing it to climb over satin stitches without jamming.

The width of the zigzag satin stitch you use will depend on the weight and size of the appliqué piece you are working with. I adjust the width of the stitch to the appliqué size: the smaller the piece, the narrower the width of the stitch.

Work slowly at first until you are comfortable zigzag satin stitching. When I appliqué, I position my fingers close to each side of the presser foot on the fabric; this gives me maximum control to turn, move, and guide the fabric as I stitch. After years of appliquéing, I still stitch slowly around small pieces. Sometimes, I stitch over a design a second time to make it look more satiny. Cotton thread fills in much better than polyester thread. You may choose to set the zigzag stitch for far apart the first time, then go over it a second time with a closer stitch. This is a very durable way to appliqué.

Use embroidery scissors to carefully trim any "shaggy" areas.

Hand Appliqué

Hand appliqué gives shapes a sculptured, softer look. It is more fragile and less durable than machine appliqué stitching, so I only recommend it on items made for special occasions. Add ⅛" to ¼" all around appliqué pattern. Where one piece is tucked under another, increase allowance to ½". You can pin appliqués in place or hand baste them if there are several pieces. Fold under seam allowances with your fingers as you go. It isn't necessary to have all edges turned or pressed under before you begin — it's too frustrating. Small, blind hemming stitches will hold pieces in place best.

Machine Quilting

Baste top, batting, and backing together. If it is a small area, pins can hold the layers in place. Set your machine to straight stitch with approximately 10 stitches per inch. Machine stitch ¼" from the stitching or sew right in the seam (stitch in the ditch). Continually check the backing or lining — sometimes it will pucker because of the loft of the batting. I place both my hands flat on each side of the presser foot and gently guide the fabric. The best way to prevent the layers from creeping is to use a walking foot, available from your sewing machine dealer. When finished with a section, pull top thread to the back and knot securely. Thread ends through a needle, hand stitch 2" to 3" away, then clip threads. Start each section in the middle and always stitch toward the outside edges, since the lining can move as you stitch.

Hand Quilting

The soft "loving hands" look of a hand-quilted garment shows that time and care went into each stitch.

Baste the three layers together, the same as for machine quilting. I prefer the strong durability of quilting thread and it won't tangle as much. A hoop or small frame is optional to hold your project taut. Knot a single thread, 18" long. Quilting needles are very sharp and move through fabrics more easily than standard sewing needles. A thimble is optional.

Outline quilt the layers of fabric together to highlight the shape of the design. Sew directly on top of the seam line or close to each side of it, using thread to match or blend with the fabric. Catch all layers with each stitch, using a small running stitch. Knot on the wrong side and slip the needle horizontally through the lining; cut thread close to lining fabric.

Hand-quilting stitches can also be placed parallel to a seam, or you may want to quilt a design in a "blank" area.

Machine Basting

If you baste or sew gathering stitches by machine, set the machine for a long straight stitch and loosen the tension slightly. Then pull the bobbin thread, either to gather the fabric or to remove basting stitches when seam is completed.

An even easier way to machine gather is to zigzag over a cord; then pull the cord to gather material, removing the cord after gathers are stitched in place.

HELPFUL HINTS

For the best results when laundering acrylic sweaters that have been appliquéd or trimmed, be sure to turn the sweaters inside-out to protect them.

I always had mixed feelings as my children grew: it meant that I could have a wonderful time making them new clothes to wear, but it also meant that the clothes I loved were not going to be worn any more. There are some great solutions, though, to the outgrown-clothing problem.

There is a lot of built-in growing room in children's clothing, especially if you make it yourself. Add extra length to the hems of jumpers, pants, and so on, so you can let down hems as children grow. Also keep in mind that a jumper is not always a jumper — it can also be a pinafore. Use it as a top over a pair of simple pants to make a charming outfit and give the jumper an added lifespan. Or, an outgrown jumper can become a sundress, with coordinating bloomers underneath. Trim the bloomers with a small appliqué that matches the jumper and you have a charming outfit for another season.

My daughter had a pair of appliquéd Oshkosh overalls that she loved to wear and was heartbroken when they were too short. I just added an elastic casing to the bottom hems and they became knickers. We added a pair of red and white striped kneesocks, and she fell in love with the outfit all over again. Because of the growing room that was built into the straps, her overalls could be worn for another year.

When clothing is just *too* small, lend them to a friend with children who wear smaller sizes. Because of the sturdy quality of the clothing you have made, they will look great for a long time. Sharing hand-me-downs will increase the value of the clothing you made, and they'll be viewed by the recipients as treasures, rather than old clothes.

After you've shared the clothes, and they've been returned, you can recycle them into a crazy quilt by cutting around the appliquéd sections and arranging them into an eye-appealing design. Piece them together, add a border, and back the quilt with a complementary fabric. Your crazy quilt will also be a memory quilt; you'll have a special time with your children, recalling all the fun they had wearing the clothes.

CHAPTER 2

Springtime Splendor:
Little Lambs 'n' Ivy

As spring approaches, a wonderful pastel palette of vibrant, fresh colors comes to mind. The Springtime Splendor set takes advantage of the wealth of that palette, while the whimsy of birds, sunshine, flowers, bunnies, and lambs brings it to life. You can create finery from top (button and ribbon barrettes) to toe (socks stenciled or trimmed to match the ensemble).

APPLIQUÉD AND QUILTED JACKET

Choose a simple, basic jacket pattern with no darts. The jacket shown in Figs. 2-1 and 2-2 has only four pattern pieces: front, back, sleeve, and band collar. The back of the jacket is a spring scene appliquéd with lambs and flowers, lightly quilted along the contours of the fields. The front of the jacket is trimmed with a perky pocket and all edges are finished with contrasting wide bias tape and jumbo rickrack trim. The right sleeve is appliquéd with a heart flower that is lightly quilted and both cuffs of the sleeves are edged with ruffled eyelet, pink mini-dot ribbon and jumbo rickrack.

Instructions are given for the girl's version, along with an adaptation of the jacket for a young boy. The jacket shown was made in a child's size 4, but the appliqués can be arranged to accommodate up to a size 12.

- Cost of materials: $16.50
- Retail cost: $75.00

Materials
Purchased simple jacket pattern
Periwinkle blue poplin, per pattern
1–1½ yards Thermolam batting (depends on size)
White with blue dot glazed cotton blend for lining, per pattern
1–2 packages extra-wide hot pink bias tape
3 yards jumbo green rickrack
1 yard 1"-wide gathered eyelet lace trim
1 yard ⅜"-wide hot pink mini-dot grosgrain ribbon
1 package single-fold white bias tape

Fig. 2–1 Little Lambs 'n' Ivy Jacket.

Fig. 2–2 Back of quilted and appliquéd jacket.

12

4 white ⅝" heart buttons
1 package lightweight iron-on interfacing
Scraps of:
    light blue heart print fabric
    large square light blue gingham
    light green pastel print fabric
    bright yellow, hot pink, and green poplin
    white piqué
    black mini-dot fabric
    white with blue floral print fabric
    light blue and pink ⅛"-wide satin ribbon
Embroidery floss in light blue, hot pink, and bright yellow
Water-soluble marking pen
Matching threads

Directions

1. Cut out front, back, sleeves and collar from periwinkle blue poplin, Thermolam batting and white with blue dot lining fabric.

2. Following general how-to instructions, trace patterns for back appliqué scene. Cut out and overlay field pieces. Note dotted lines on outer ends of field pieces: these can be extended or shortened to fit jacket back as needed. If darker fabrics are showing through lighter ones, back light fabric with lightweight iron-on interfacing. Back white piqué, black mini-dot fabric, pink, yellow, and green poplin scraps with lightweight iron-on interfacing before cutting out appliqués.

Cut out appliqué pieces as follows:

1 sun: yellow poplin
2 clouds: white with blue floral print
5 hearts: hot pink poplin
8 leaves: green poplin
2 lamb bodies: white piqué
2 lamb faces, 2 ears, 2 pair front legs, and 2 pair back legs: black mini-dot fabric

Note: Some pieces should be cut in reverse, as indicated on the pattern piece.

3. Pin three field pieces to jacket back with outer edges meeting jacket sides and bottom edge, overlapping per placement drawing. Using wide zigzag satin stitch, appliqué pieces starting with A, then B, and finally C. Trim edges evenly as needed.

4. Pin clouds and sun in sky, with sun peeking out of right lower cloud. Appliqué in place with medium-width zigzag satin stitch. Using water-soluble marking pen, draw in eyes, nose, mouth, and sun rays. Using two strands of embroidery

floss, embroider face as follows: satin stitch eyes with light blue floss; straight stitch eyebrows with light blue floss; satin stitch nose with pink floss; back stitch mouth with pink floss; and back stitch sun rays with yellow floss.

5. Pin lamb shapes per placement drawing (if making a larger size, space them for a pleasing arrangement). Tuck faces, front legs, and back legs under white piqué body. Using medium-width zigzag satin stitch, appliqué around lamb bodies. With narrow zigzag satin stitch, appliqué faces, front legs, and back legs. Position and appliqué ears. Embroider light blue eyes on lamb faces with two strands of light blue embroidery floss, using satin stitch or french knot. Tie tiny bows in pink and light blue from ⅛"-wide satin ribbon and tack under lambs' faces.

6. Position hearts and leaves as shown on pattern placement guide and pin (space out as needed for large size jacket). Appliqué all hearts with medium-width zigzag satin stitch; then appliqué leaves with medium-width stitch also.

7. Layer jacket back pieces with lining facing right-side-down, batting in middle, and appliquéd back piece facing right-side-up. Pin and machine baste around perimeter of piece, ⅛" from edge. Hand baste piece as shown in Diag. 2-1 (see pattern section at end of chapter for all diagrams).

8. The jacket shown was hand quilted. Hand or machine quilt around upper left cloud; around lower right cloud and sun face; across top of field piece A above satin stitch; just above satin stitching of field piece C, going around bottom of lamb and down to bottom edge of jacket; and across field piece B above satin stitching, over top of lamb and up to jacket side. Remove hand basting stitches across jacket back and set aside.

9. Cut out heart and leaves for right sleeve from pink and green poplin, respectively. Poplin should be backed with lightweight iron-on interfacing before cutting. Pin heart and leaves to mid-upper center of right sleeve and appliqué, using medium-width zigzag satin stitch. Straight topstitch vein in leaf, per pattern. Layer sleeve with lining right-side-down, batting in middle, and appliquéd sleeve facing right-side-up. Pin and machine baste around perimeter of sleeve, ⅛" from edge. Hand baste a circle around heart flower and either hand or machine quilt. Pull quilting thread slightly to give a little puff to heart flower. Remove hand basting stitches around flower. Layer other sleeve with lining right-side-down, batting in middle, and blue poplin right-side-up. Pin and machine baste ⅛" from perimeter around sleeve. Set sleeves aside.

10. Layer front pieces as described before; machine baste around perimeters, ⅛" from edge. Be sure to have one right front and one left front when layering.

11. With right sides together, pin shoulder seams of fronts to back piece; seam, using ⅝" seam allowance. Trim and grade seams to ¼" and press open. Cut two pieces single-fold white bias tape to length of shoulder seam. Pin; then

blind stitch edges of bias tape over shoulder seam by hand, being careful not to stitch through to right side of jacket. Lightly press.

12. Gather, pin, and stitch sleeve caps to jacket, per purchased pattern instructions. Restitch seam $^1/_{16}$″ inside first seam. Grade and trim seam to ¼″ to ease bulkiness.

13. To trim sleeve cuffs, stitch 1″-wide gathered eyelet lace trim across bottom edge of cuffs, with eyelet facing up. Unfold one edge of white single-fold bias tape and stitch on fold over edge of eyelet lace binding. Fold and press edge of bias tape so sleeve edge is eyelet lace trimmed; blind stitch bias tape to sleeve lining by hand, being careful not to stitch through to blue poplin. On right side of sleeve, stitch jumbo green rickrack ⅛″ above eyelet lace. Baste pink mini-dot grosgrain ribbon between eyelet lace and jumbo green rickrack so only top edge of rickrack points show. Stitch on both edges of pink ribbon. Repeat for other sleeve.

14. Pin underarm side seams and stitch, using ⅝″ seam allowance. Grade and trim seams to ¼″ and press open. Cut two pieces of single-fold white bias tape to fit side seam from underarm to bottom. Pin; blind stitch edges of bias tape over side seams by hand, being careful not to stitch through to blue poplin.

15. Layer collar as previously described; pin and machine baste ⅛″ from perimeter of collar. Following purchased pattern instructions, attach collar. Grade and trim seam allowances to ¼″, press open, and finish seam, blind stitching single-fold white bias tape over seam by hand.

16. Starting at side seam, stitch jumbo green rickrack around entire perimeter of jacket, ⅛″ from edge. Encase front sides, collar, and back of jacket with hot pink extra-wide bias tape by starting at underarm seam, unfolding wide edge of tape, and pin around perimeter. Stitch on fold line so that, when bias tape is folded over to encase edge, only top points of jumbo green rickrack show. Fold over bias tape and blind stitch to lining side by hand, being careful not to stitch through to right side of jacket. Press.

17. Cut two pockets from periwinkle blue poplin and 1 pocket from Thermolam batting. Cut heart and leaves from pink and green poplin that has been backed with lightweight iron-on interfacing. Pin and appliqué heart flower per pattern piece, using medium-width zigzag satin stitch. Stitch jumbo green rickrack ¾″ from pocket top. Position pink mini-dot grosgrain ribbon so only bottom points of rickrack show. Stitch bottom edge of pink dot ribbon. Tuck gathered edge of 1″-wide gathered eyelet lace trim under top edge of pink dot ribbon, tucking under edges ⅜″ from each side. Stitch top edge of pink dot ribbon. Fold eyelet trim down over pink dot ribbon and rickrack and pin. Layer pocket with batting on bottom, plain blue poplin lining right-side-up, and appliquéd pocket piece facing right-side-down. Pin pocket and stitch ¼″ from edge around sides and bottom, leaving top open. Turn right-side-out, unpin eyelet lace so it faces up, turn

under top back of pocket ¼″ and hand stitch closed. Hand quilt around heart flower, pulling quilted thread slightly so it gives a little puff to heart flower. Position and pin pocket on left front side of jacket, as shown in Fig. 2-1. Topstitch around U shape of pocket ⅛″ from edge.

18. Position four white heart buttons, evenly spaced down right side of jacket front; mark with water-soluble marking pen. Sew on buttons at marking. Make corresponding machine or hand buttonholes on left front side.

Boy's Jacket Adaptation

1. Fields, clouds, sun, and lambs remain as shown for jacket back (Fig. 2-2). Refer to boy's shortall for spring and cut out three trees, to be arranged in a group of two on right side with one on left side of fields. Purchase five bunny buttons in pastel colors (can be other animal buttons if you prefer) and stitch to woodland scene randomly.

2. Change heart flower on sleeve to yellow poplin star. Outline quilt lightly, pulling thread slightly to puff star. Omit eyelet/ribbon/rickrack trim from sleeve cuffs. Edge sleeves with yellow piping; finish cuffs with white single-fold bias tape by hemming to lining of sleeve.

3. Use yellow poplin star appliqué for pocket, instead of heart flower. Omit eyelet/ribbon/rickrack trim, and edge entire perimeter of pocket with yellow piping. Complete pocket as instructed. Lightly quilt star. Position, pin, and sew pocket to jacket, topstitching around U shape, ⅛″ from edge.

4. Change heart buttons to ⅝″ white star buttons down jacket front.

5. Edge jacket with yellow piping and finish hem with white single-fold bias tape, folding and blind stitching hem to lining of side of jacket.

APPLIQUÉD JUMPER

The versatile jumper shown in Fig. 2-3 can be dressed up with a white blouse, or double for summer fun as a sundress.

- Cost of materials: $9.00
- Retail cost: $25.00

Materials
Purchased pattern for jumper with squared bodice and gathered skirt
¼ yard each bright yellow and hot pink poplin
½ yard periwinkle blue poplin for jumper skirt
  (based on child's size 4; adjust fabric amounts for size)
2 yards 1″-wide pink gingham ribbon
1 package lightweight iron-on interfacing
Scraps of:
  large-check light blue gingham
  light green pastel print fabric

16

*Fig. 2–3 Little Lambs 'n'
Ivy appliquéd jumper and
shortall.*

green poplin
white piqué
black mini-dot fabric
white with light blue floral print fabric
⅛"-wide pink satin ribbon
2 light blue bird buttons
Matching threads

Directions

1. Cut two bib backs (1 back plus lining) from pink poplin. Cut two bib fronts from yellow poplin (1 front plus lining). Do not cut shoulder straps; pink gingham ribbon ties will be substituted. Cut skirt, per purchased pattern, from periwinkle blue poplin.

2. Back pink poplin, green poplin, white piqué, black mini-dot fabric, and white with blue print fabric scraps with lightweight iron-on interfacing. Following general how-to instructions, trace patterns for appliquéd bib front. Cut out and overlay field pieces. These can be shortened or extended to fit bib front as need-

17

ed. If darker fabric is showing through lighter field piece, back light field piece with lightweight iron-on interfacing. Appliqué field pieces in place, using wide zigzag satin stitch.

3. Cut appliqué pieces for scene:

1 cloud: white with light blue floral print
2 hearts: hot pink poplin
4 leaves: green poplin
1 lamb body: white piqué
1 lamb face, 1 lamb ear, 1 pair front legs, and 1 pair back legs: black mini-dot fabric

4. Appliqué scene in the following order, using medium-width zigzag satin stitch: position and pin cloud in right sky per pattern placement drawing; appliqué. Position and pin heart flowers in right field and appliqué in place. Position and pin lamb body in left field as shown; tuck head, front legs, and back legs under white piqué body. Appliqué lamb body, then face, front legs, and back legs. Position ear and appliqué.

5. Tie tiny bow, using ⅛"-wide pink satin ribbon and tack under lamb's head. Sew bird buttons in sky. Press.

6. Cut pink gingham ribbon into four 18" lengths. Position one at each marking where shoulder strap would go on purchased pattern. Pin appliquéd bib front to bib lining, with right sides together, and stitch using ⅝" seam allowance across armholes and bib top to other armhole. Trim seam allowance to ¼". Be sure not to sew side seams. Turn right-side-out and press.

7. With ribbon shoulder straps pinned to back bib piece, pin bib back to bib back lining (right sides together). Stitch armhole, across bib back top and second armhole, using ⅝" seam allowance. Do not sew side seams. Trim seam allowance to ¼", turn, and press. Cut all ribbon shoulder strap ends into a V shape.

8. Pin pink bib back to yellow appliquéd bib front at side seams, right sides together, and stitch, using ⅝" seam allowance. Trim to ¼" seam allowance and press.

9. With right sides together, pin and sew blue poplin skirt side seams, using ⅝" seam allowances. Press seams open.

10. Gather skirt along waist to fit bib top, matching side seams. Baste skirt to bib top, adjusting gathers to fit evenly. Stitch, using ⅝" seam allowance. Fold under bib linings ½" and hand hem bib lining to skirt waist. Press. Hem skirt per pattern instructions. Press.

11. Tie bows at shoulders.

As child outgrows the jumper, use as a sundress, with an eyelet-edged petticoat underneath, just peeking out, for an especially pretty country look.

APPLIQUÉD SHORTALL

The boy's shortall is shown with the jumper in Fig. 2-3.

- Cost of materials: $10.00
- Retail Cost: $25.00

Materials

1 purchased shortall pattern with contrasting front bodice
⅜ yard bright yellow poplin
¼ yard green poplin
⅝ yard periwinkle blue poplin
   (for child's size 4; check pattern instructions for amount of shorts fabric)
1 package lightweight iron-on interfacing
Scraps of:
   white with light blue floral print fabric
   large-check light blue gingham
   light blue heart print fabric
   light green pastel print fabric
   green dot fabric
   white piqué
   black mini-dot fabric
   pink ⅛"-wide satin ribbon
Light blue embroidery floss
2 white ½" star buttons
3 bunny buttons (1 yellow, 1 pink, 1 lavender)
2 frog buttons
1 light blue bird button
Matching threads

Directions

1. Cut 2 bodice fronts from yellow poplin (1 front bib plus lining). Cut shoulder straps from green poplin and back bib lining from green poplin. Cut back and front of shorts from periwinkle blue poplin.

2. Back the following fabrics with lightweight iron-on interfacing: white with light blue floral print fabric; green dot fabric; white piqué; and black mini-dot fabric. Following general how-to instructions, trace patterns for appliquéd bodice front. Cut out and overlay field pieces; these may be shortened or extended to fit bodice front as needed. If darker fabric is showing through lighter field piece, back lighter fabric with lightweight iron-on interfacing. Appliqué field pieces in place, using wide zigzag satin stitch.

3. Cut appliqué pieces for scene:

1 cloud: white with light blue floral print
1 tree: green dot fabric
1 lamb body: white piqué
1 lamb face, 1 ear, 1 pair front legs, and 1 pair back legs: black mini-dot
   fabric

4. Use medium-width zigzag satin stitch to appliqué the scene pieces, follow pattern placement drawing to stitch in this order: cloud in right sky; tree on right side of field; lamb body on left side of field, with head, front legs, and back legs tucked under body; lamb face; lamb front legs; lamb back legs; lamb ear. Embroider lamb eye with light blue embroidery floss, and tie a little bow using pink ⅛" satin ribbon, tacking bow under lamb head.

5. Sew bunny buttons around bottom of tree, as shown in Fig. 2-3. Sew light blue bird button in sky.

6. Following purchased pattern instructions, complete shortall. If shortall pattern has side closure, use frog buttons. If the pattern does not have side buttons, stitch frog buttons into scene on each side. Use white star buttons for buttoning shoulder straps.

CARDIGAN SWEATERS FOR SPRING

Spring weather is often fickle and a cardigan sweater is the perfect answer to a brisk spring breeze. By slightly changing a purchased white acrylic cardigan, you can create a designer delight (see color section).

- Cost of materials: $12.00
- Retail cost: $22.00

Materials for Girl's Sweater
   1 purchased white acrylic cardigan sweater
   7 pink ½" heart buttons
   ¾ yard 1"-wide white satin picot ribbon
   4" of ⅝"-wide bright green grosgrain ribbon
   Matching threads

Directions
   1. Cut off buttons originally on sweater and put aside. Replace with pink heart buttons.

2. Loop ribbon, per Diag. 2-2, to make six-loop bow; tack in center. Stitch short ends of green grosgrain ribbon together and gather inner edge to form rosette. Pull thread tightly and knot securely. Stitch remaining pink heart button to center of green grosgrain rosette; glue rosette to center of six-loop bow (Diag. 2-3).

3. Place fancy bow on upper right side of sweater; tack in place from the wrong side.

20

Springtime Splendor:
Little Lambs 'n' Ivy

Fig. 1 Clockwise, from top center: Lambs 'n' Ivy basket, purchased cardigan dressed up for Spring, beribboned barrettes, and girl's and boy's kneesocks, stenciled and stitched for coordinating accessories.

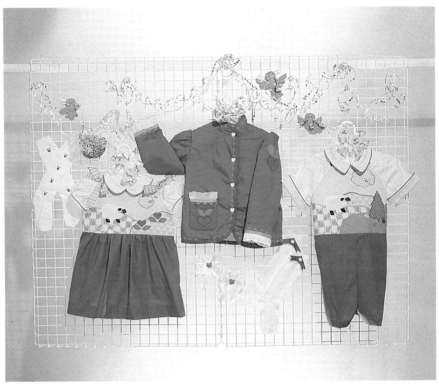

Fig. 2 Appliquéd jumper, jacket, and shortall. Garments are constructed from simple patterns; instructions are given in Chapter 2 for all Spring items.

Fig. 3 Back view of appliquéd and quilted jacket (front shown in Fig. 2).

Summer Splash: Beach Bear Buddies

Fig. 4 Teddy bear tote takes to the beach here, but can be decorated for any season. Shown on rubber raft are the Bear-y Special Bikini and Funky Feet Thongs.

Fig. 5 Inexpensive
sweatshirts go from plain
to pizzazz with the addi-
tion of easy teddy appli-
qués. Boy's cover-up
shown with teddy trunks
and thongs; girl's cover-
up shown with bikini
bottom and trimmed
thongs. Quick and easy
Summer project direc-
tions provided in Chap-
ter 3.

Fig. 6 Boy's teddy motif
shows up on purchased
shirt, and on shorts that
can be made or bought.
Hooded bear towel for
warming up is shown
here in girl's version, but
directions are given for a
boy's variation, too.

Americana Autumn: Back to School

Fig. 7 No wardrobe is complete without a snazzy sweater or two. Directions are provided in Chapter 4 for transforming ordinary crewnecks and cardigans into designer duds with the simple addition of appliqués and trims.

Fig. 8 Animal Crackers vest, jumper, and pants are constructed from easy commercial patterns, then given the cachet of designer togs with charming appliqués. Purchased crewneck sports a coordinating motif to complete favorite back-to-school outfits; directions for all in Chapter 4.

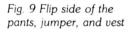

Fig. 9 Flip side of the pants, jumper, and vest

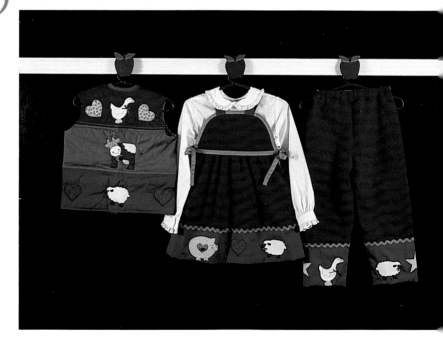

Winter Wonderland: Visions of Sugarplums

Fig. 10 Dressed for the holidays, a little girl will wear a smiling snowman on her jumper – and carry an adorable matching purse! Not to be outdone, a favorite fellow shows off in personalized pants and reindeer sweater – and carries a durable, go-everywhere reindeer duffle bag. Directions for all are found in Chapter 5.

Fig. 11 Santa thought of everything this year. For toasty warmth, you can't beat reindeer- and bear-adorned hats, mittens, gloves, and scarves. A Christmas goose adorns a special sweater; a bear family decorates the stockings for boys and girls; and an easy-to-make teddy toy coordinates with appliquéd nightshirt.

Fig. 12 The Sunbonnet Angel Pinafore will dress your little angel in classic elegance. Perfect to wear over velveteen for special holidays, or make full-length for a summer wedding.

Materials for Boy's Sweater

    1 purchased white acrylic cardigan sweater
    7 yellow ⅝″ sun buttons
    4″ of ⅝″-wide periwinkle blue grosgrain ribbon
    Matching threads

Directions

    1. Cut off buttons originally on sweater and put aside. Replace with yellow sun buttons.
    2. Tie knot in center of blue grosgrain ribbon and stitch sun button in center of knot (Diag. 2-4). Cut ends of ribbon into V shapes.
    3. Place tie on upper right side of sweater; tack from wrong side.

BUTTON AND RIBBON BARRETTES

    The completed barettes are shown in the color insert.

- Cost of materials: $1.50
- Retail cost: $6.00

Materials

    1 pair Goody barrettes
    1½ yards ⅝″-wide white satin picot ribbon
    ¼ yard ⅛″-wide light blue satin ribbon
    2 hot pink ¾″ heart buttons
    Hot glue stick and hot glue gun
    Matching threads

Directions

    1. Cut white picot ribbon in half. Loop ribbon to make six-loop bow (see Diag. 2-2). Tack bow in center. Stitch pink heart button to center of bow. Repeat for second bow. Cut ⅛″-wide light blue satin ribbon in half and tie two tiny bows. Glue a blue bow to center of each heart button (Diag. 2-5).
    2. Open barrette and stitch bow to middle top of barrette. Glue underside of bow to barrette bar to secure. Repeat for second barrette.

GIRL'S KNEESOCKS

    The stenciled socks are shown in Fig. 2-4.

- Cost of materials: $.75
- Retail cost: $6.00

Materials

    1 pair white nylon kneesocks
    Pink acrylic paint
    Green acrylic paint

#001 sable paintbrush
Tagboard or shirt cardboard
Water-soluble marking pen

Directions

1. Cut piece of tagboard or shirt cardboard to slip into kneesocks without stretching sock. This will absorb any extra paint that may seep through painted side of sock.

2. With water-soluble marking pen, mark four dots evenly spaced down outside of leg for heart flower placement.

3. Following pattern in Diag. 2-6, either stencil or paint freehand heart flowers, with pink hearts and green leaves. Allow to dry one hour

4. Using pressing cloth, steam press over socks to set paints permanently.

Variation of Girl's Kneesocks

Another special touch for a pair of kneesocks is to make smaller versions of fancy ribbon-looped bows, just like the ones for the barrettes. Tack these to outer top of kneesocks just under elastic band.

Fig. 2–4 Lambs 'n' Ivy Basket and girl's and boy's kneesocks.

BOY'S KNEESOCKS

The boy's kneesocks are shown in Fig. 2-4.

- Cost of materials: $1.25
- Retail cost: $6.00

Materials

1 pair white nylon kneesocks
2 yellow sun buttons
6" of ⅝"-wide periwinkle blue grosgrain ribbon
Matching threads

Directions

1. Cut blue ribbon into two 3" pieces. Tie into knot in center, per Diagram 2-4, and stitch sun button to center of knot. Cut ends of ribbon into V shapes.

2. Position tie at outer top of kneesock, just below ribbing. Tack from wrong side. Repeat for other sock.

LAMBS 'N' IVY BASKET

The basket, shown in Fig. 2-4, is a perfect complement to the Springtime Splendor set.

- Cost of materials: $10.00
- Retail cost: $25.00

Materials

1 round wicker basket, approximately 10" high x 10" wide
1½ yards ⅜"-wide pink mini-dot grosgrain ribbon
⅞ yards 1"-wide gathered eyelet lace trim
⅜ yard 45"-wide light blue heart-striped print fabric
⅓ yard 2"-wide white cluny lace
Scraps of white, pink, light blue, and black felt
6" of ⅛"-wide pink satin ribbon
White mohair yarn
1 black pipecleaner
¼" brass bell
Pink and light blue nosegay flowers
Polyfil stuffing
Hot glue sticks and hot glue gun
Matching threads

Directions

1. Cut light blue heart-striped fabric into two strips, 6¾" wide by 45" long. With right sides together, seam short ends with ¼" seam allowance to make con-

tinuous length 6¾" by 89½". Fold top 2½" to wrong side and press. For hem, fold bottom ¼" to wrong side, press and machine stitch hem.

2. Gather ruffle 2" down from top fold. Adjust gathers evenly to fit basket and securely tie threads. If you have trouble with ruffle slipping, use clothespins to hold in place.

3. Cut pink dot grosgrain ribbon to fit around basket ruffle with ½" overlap, and set aside. With remaining ribbon, start at one end of handle and glue ribbon at place where handle meets basket. Wrap handle with ribbon to other handle side and glue at other end to secure.

4. Glue ruffle along gathered line to basket rim with hot glue gun. Glue 1"-wide gathered eyelet lace trim over gathering line, overlapping ends neatly. Finish ruffle by gluing hot pink mini-dot grosgrain ribbon over eyelet binding, overlapping ends for finished look.

5. Sew short ends of white cluny lace together to make continuous tube, using ¼" seam allowance. Gather on inner edge and pull tightly to make gathered oval. Knot securely and set aside.

6. Cut two lamb bodies from white felt and two lamb faces and two lamb ears from black felt. Pin and stitch around lamb body with ¼" seam allowance, leaving opening as indicated on pattern. Turn and stuff body with polyfil stuffing. Hand stitch body closed. Stitch around lamb face with ⅛" seam allowance, leaving opening indicated on pattern. Turn, stuff face, and hand stitch to upper left side of lamb body. Tack ears to sides of head, pinching them slightly so they stick up. Cut tiny triangle from pink felt for nose and glue in place. Cut tiny dots of light blue felt for eyes and glue in place (Diag. 2-7).

7. Cut piece of black felt, 4" long by ⅝" wide. Put 4" piece of black pipecleaner on lengthwise center of black felt and stitch lengthwise down side, encasing pipecleaner. Cut pipecleaner/felt piece into four 1"-long pieces. Glue these "legs" to underside of lamb body with hot glue gun.

8. Using white mohair yarn, wrap around little finger 3 times. Slip off and hand stitch loops through the center to lamb body; repeat until entire body is thoroughly covered with fuzzy loops. Slip brass bell onto pink ⅛"-wide satin ribbon and tie bell under lamb's head, with bow on top as shown in Fig. 2-4.

9. Snip 5 pink and 3 blue nosegay flowers off at stem. Glue lamb body to center of gathered oval cluny lace. Glue nosegay flowers randomly around lamb legs. Fasten lamb decoration to bottom of basket handle with hot glue.

Spring Adaptations

• Using ruffled edges in a variety of colors makes the basket extremely versatile. You can also change the lamb decoration to a teddy bear motif, using bear shown on beach sandals in Chapter 3. Or, create a special Christmas treat decorated in red and green fabrics, trimmed with reindeer head shown in stocking stuffer section of Chapter 5.

- The pocket used on the appliquéd jacket looks darling attached to purchased sweater, pants, jumper, or sweatsuit.
- If time is at a premium, the appliquéd scene on jacket back can be appliquéd to purchased jacket. Scenes on jumper and shortall adapt well to purchased bib overalls and bib jumpers. Add bright ribbon trim to overall straps to complete look.
- Lamb appliqué alone can adorn sleepwear, sheets, pillowcases, and towels for coordinated bed and bath ensemble.

Embroidery Stitches

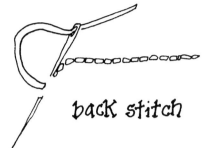

back stitch

running stitch

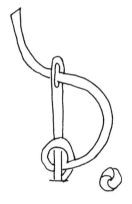

french knot

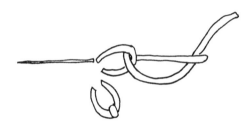

lazy daisy stitch

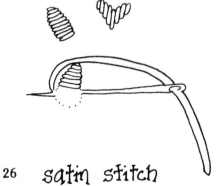

26 satin stitch

stem stitch

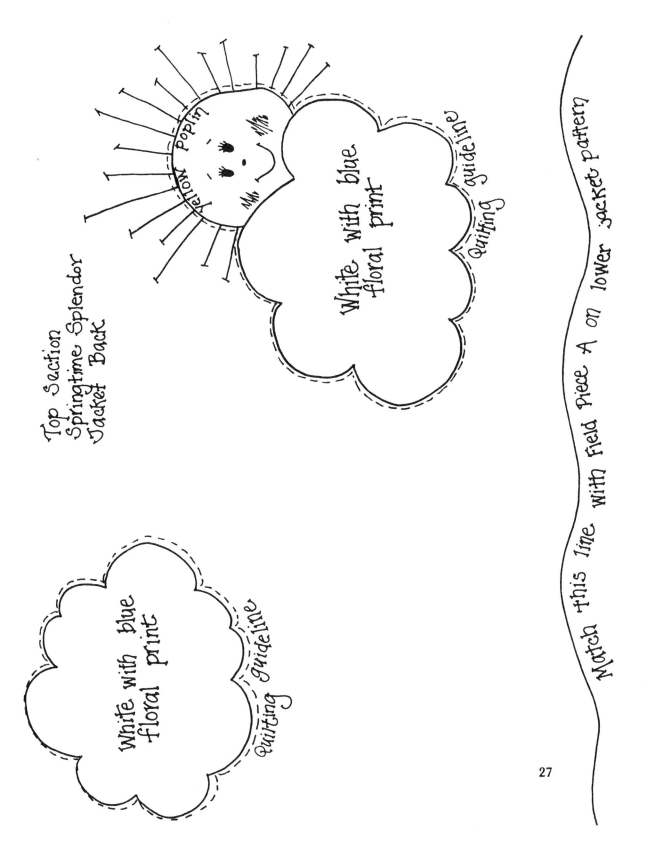

Top Section
Springtime Splendor
Jacket Back

Yellow Poplin

White with blue
floral print

Quilting guideline

White with blue
floral print

Quilting guideline

Match this line with field Piece A on lower jacket pattern

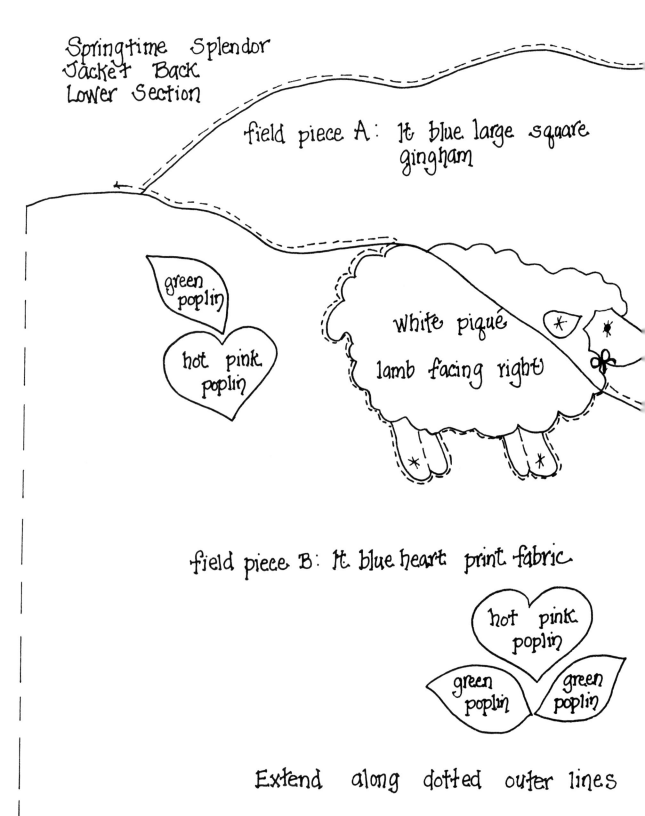

Springtime Splendor
Jacket Back
Lower Section

field piece A: lt. blue large square gingham

green poplin

hot pink poplin

white piqué
lamb facing right

field piece B: lt. blue heart print fabric

hot pink poplin

green poplin

green poplin

Extend along dotted outer lines

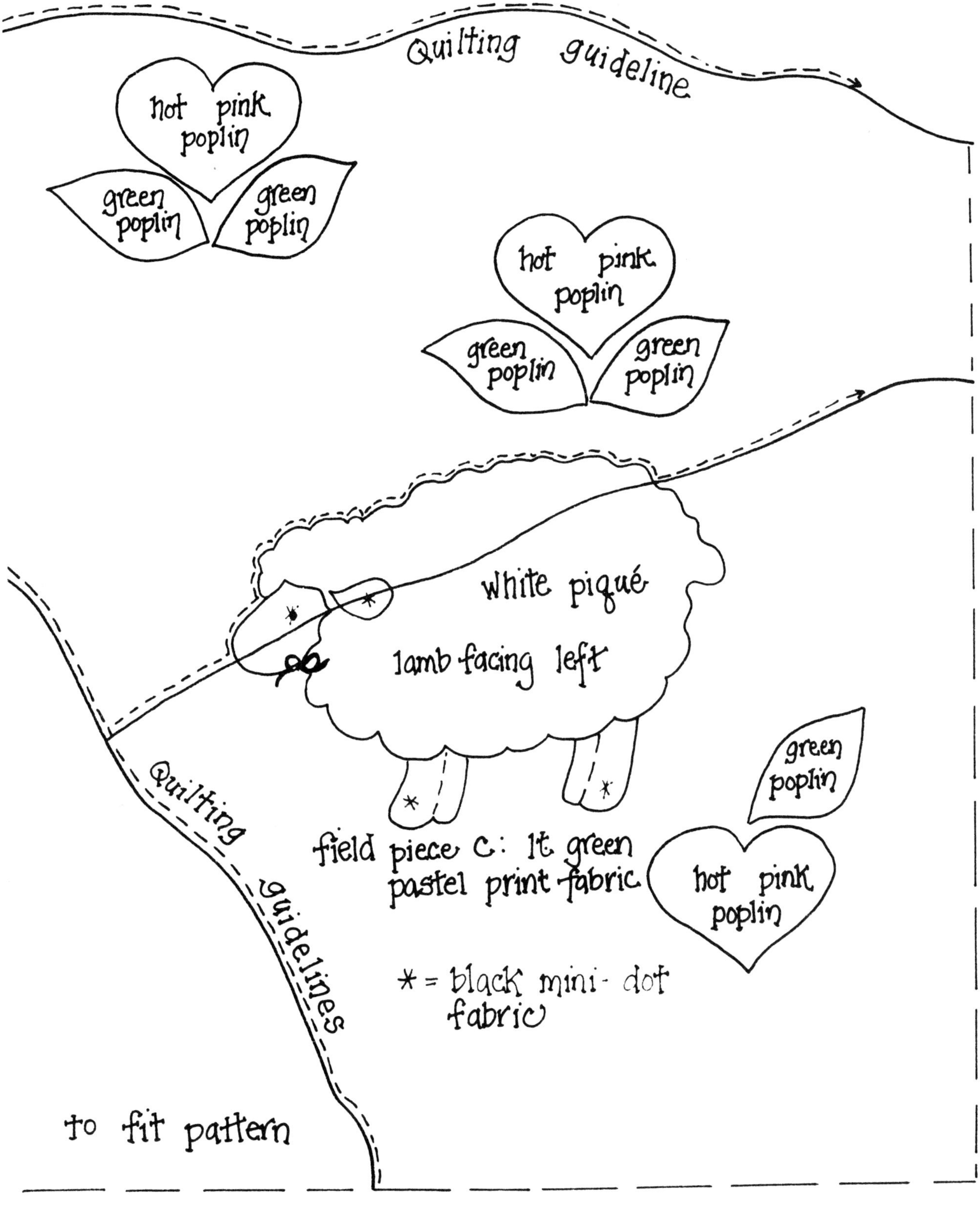

Quilting guideline
hot pink poplin
green poplin
green poplin
hot pink poplin
green poplin
green poplin
white piqué
lamb facing left
green poplin
hot pink poplin
Quilting guidelines
field piece C: lt green pastel print fabric
* = black mini-dot fabric
to fit pattern

left side cloud

cut 1

white with blue
floral print

right side cloud

cut 1

white with blue
floral print

sun - cut 1

Yellow poplin

heart
flower

Cut 5
hot pink poplin

Cut 2 - green poplin

single
leaf

double
leaf

Cut 3
green poplin

lamb body

Cut 2 (1 in reverse)

white piqué

Springtime Splendor
Jacket pattern pieces

ear

face

back
legs

front
legs

Cut 2 each (1 in reverse)
black mini-dot print

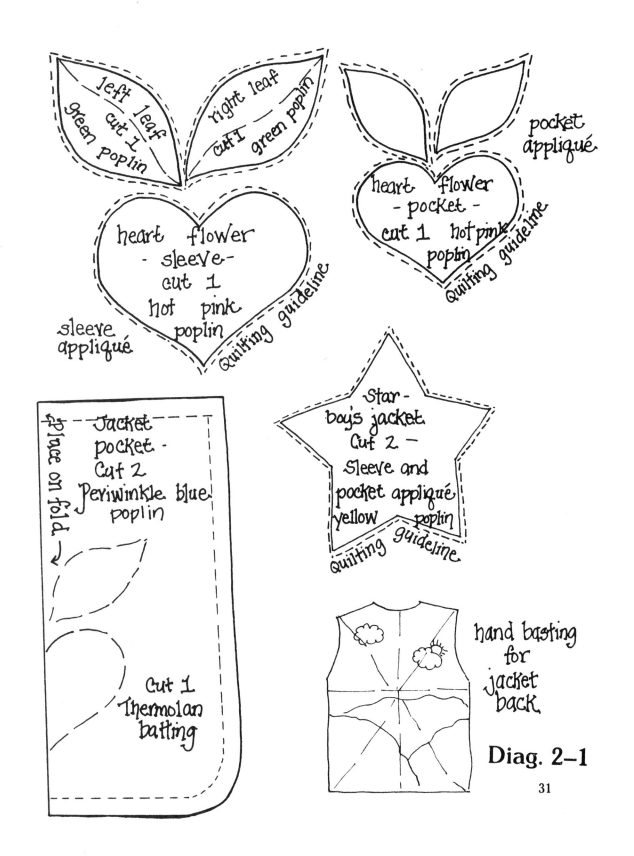

left leaf
cut 1
green poplin

right leaf
cut 1 green poplin

pocket appliqué

heart flower
- sleeve -
cut 1
hot pink
poplin

sleeve appliqué

Quilting guideline

heart flower
- pocket -
cut 1 hot pink poplin

Quilting guideline

Jacket pocket -
Cut 2
Periwinkle blue
poplin

Place on fold

Cut 1
Thermolan batting

Star -
boy's jacket
Cut 2 -
sleeve and
pocket appliqué
yellow poplin

Quilting guideline

hand basting
for
jacket
back

Diag. 2-1

31

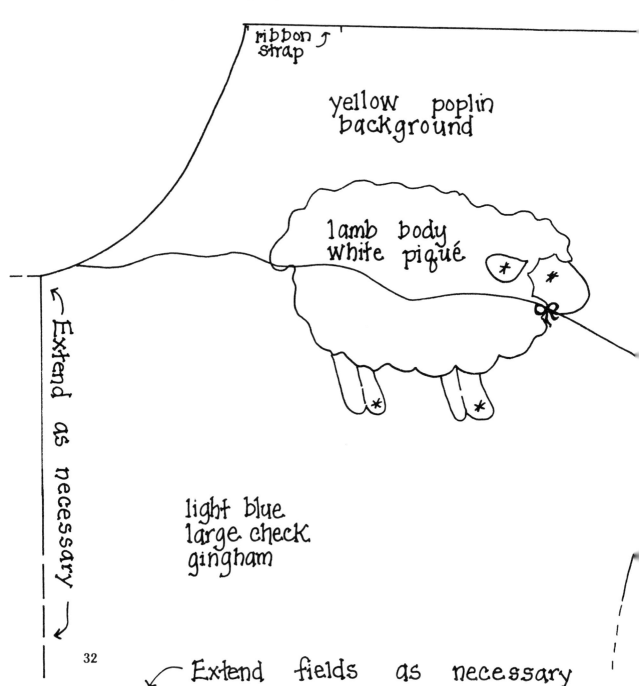

Springtime Splendor Jumper
front bodice

ribbon ↲
strap

yellow poplin
background

lamb body
white piqué

← Extend as necessary →

light blue
large check
gingham

32

↙ Extend fields as necessary

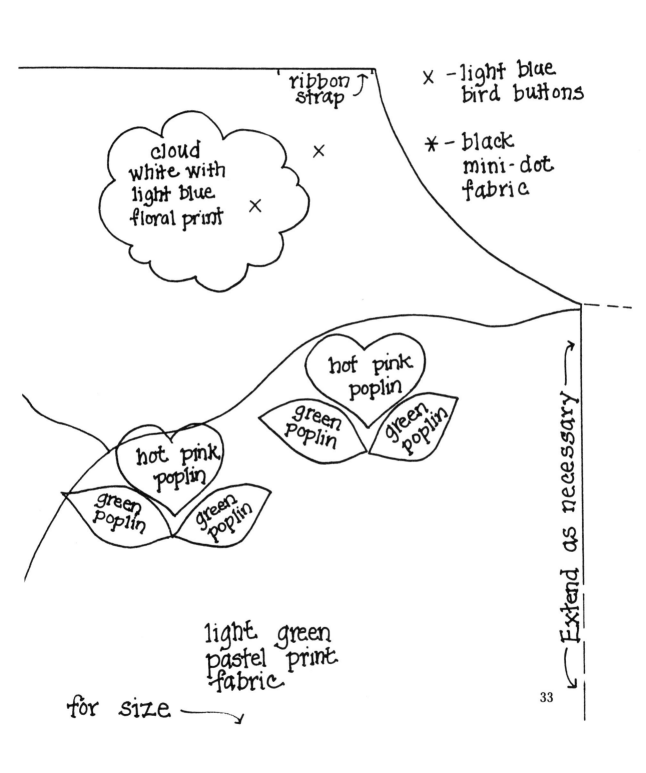

ribbon
strap

X – light blue
bird buttons

* – black
mini-dot
fabric

cloud
white with
light blue
floral print

hot pink
poplin

green
poplin

green
poplin

hot pink
poplin

green
poplin

green
poplin

Extend as necessary

light green
pastel print
fabric

for size

33

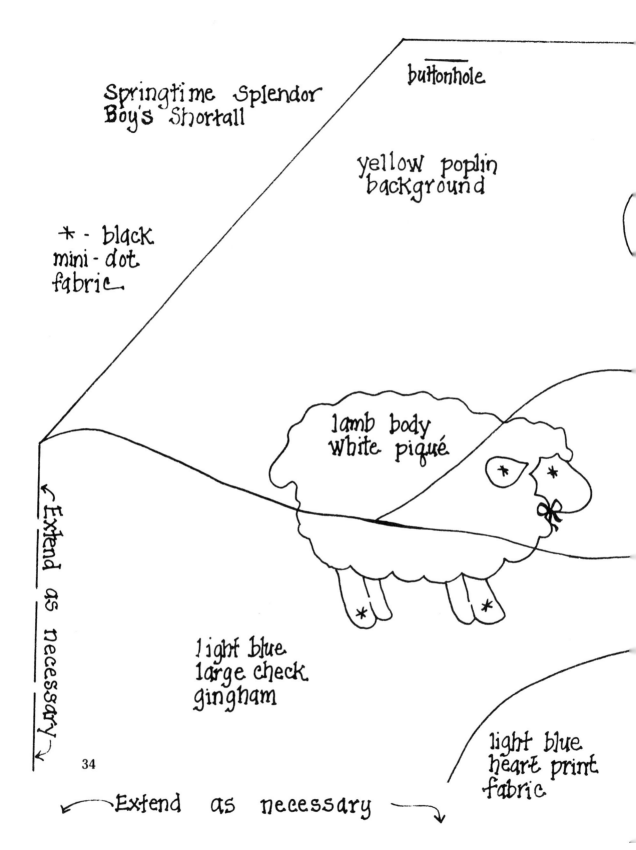

Springtime Splendor
Boy's Shortall

buttonhole

yellow poplin
background

* - black
mini - dot
fabric

lamb body
white piqué

Extend as necessary

34

light blue
large check
gingham

light blue
heart print
fabric

Extend as necessary

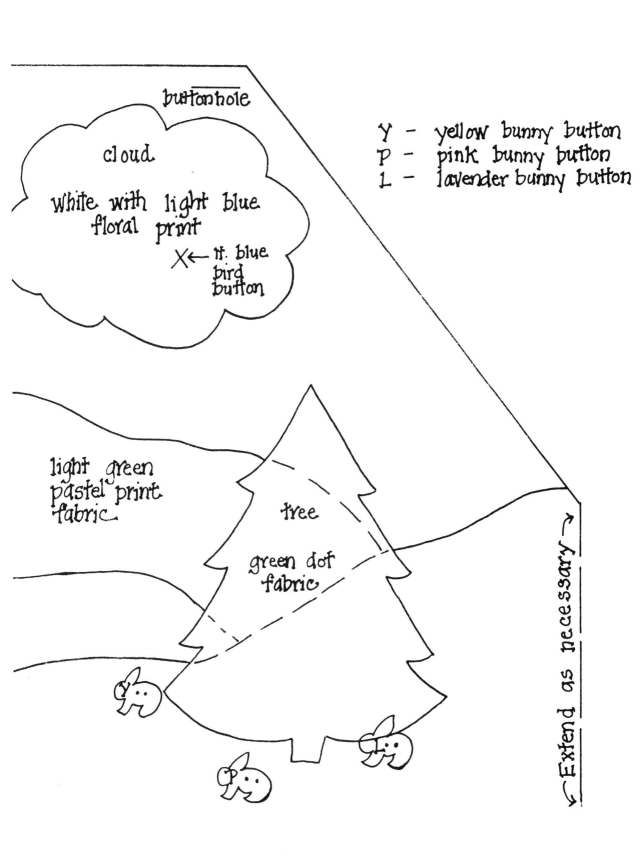

buttonhole

cloud

white with light blue floral print

X ← lt. blue bird button

Y — yellow bunny button
P — pink bunny button
L — lavender bunny button

light green pastel print fabric

tree

green dot fabric

← Extend as necessary →

To make 6-loop bow:

1. Pinch in center

Make 1 loop

2. Pinch

Add loop on right

3. Pinch

Add loop to each side

4. Add another loop to each side to make 6.

Tie tightly or sew through center to hold.

Diag. 2–2

Girl's Cardigan Sweater bow

Diag. 2–3

Barrette bow

Diag. 2–5

Boy's cardigan and Knee-socks bow

Diag. 2–4

Stencil pattern - Girl's Knee-socks

Diag. 2–6

leaves - green

heart - hot pink

lamb body cut 2 white felt

←leave open→

36

Lambs 'n Ivy Basket

Cut 2 each black felt

face

ear

detail of lamb's face

Diag. 2–7

CHAPTER 3

Summer Splash:
Beach Bear Buddies

As the days grow longer and warmer, summer shimmers on the horizon. Thoughts turn to days at the beach, picnics in the park, and lemonade stands on street corners. With glorious sunny days beckoning us outside, leisure time becomes even more precious.

All the projects in this chapter require only an evening each to accomplish, yet all are packed with plenty of pizzazz! Whether running through the sprinkler or swimming at a summer resort, your youngster will steal the show wearing this bright assortment of Beach Bear Buddies.

Most kids take to swimming lessons like a duck takes to water. My surefire barometer that it was time to come out of the pool was blue fingers and chattering teeth — even if the children clamored that they weren't the least bit cold. The appliquéd cover-ups will warm hearts on the inside and outside. The purchased sweatshirts for the Beach Bear Buddy Cover-Ups are appliquéd and trimmed with unique charm (Figs. 3-1 and 3-2).

GIRL'S COVER-UP

- Cost of materials: $9.00
- Retail cost: $35.00

Materials

1 purchased lavender sweatshirt
1 yard ¾"-wide gathered eyelet lace trim
1 yard single-fold white bias tape
1 yard ⅜"-wide hot pink mini-dot grosgrain ribbon
1 package lightweight iron-on interfacing
½ yard ¼"-wide white elastic
Scraps of:
  tan velour
  yellow and white floral print fabric
  tan with white mini-print fabric
  white pastel floral print
  light blue print fabric

Fig. 3–1 Girl's Cover-Up.

Fig. 3–2 Boy's Cover-Up.

pink print fabric
heart lace and scallop-edge lace
brown acrylic felt
Embroidery floss in yellow, pink, and light blue
Nosegay flower
4" of ¼"-wide white satin ribbon
Black acrylic paint
Water-soluble marking pen
Non-soluble tacky glue
Pink Venus pencil
Matching threads

Directions

1. Cut off sleeves to short length. If you are unsure of amount to cut, a good rule of thumb is to fold sleeve in half and cut one inch above fold. On sizes 7 and up, you can cut two inches above fold.

2. Back all fabric scraps listed with lightweight iron-on interfacing. Cut out sun and pin to middle of right sleeve. Cut a piece of lightweight iron-on interfacing slightly larger than sun appliqué and fuse to *wrong* side of sleeve under appliqué area. This procedure stabilizes the sweatshirt knit from stretching while appliqué-ing. Appliqué sun, using medium-width zigzag satin stitch. Using water-soluble marking pen, draw in sun face and sun rays, as shown on pattern. Embroider sun face using two strands of embroidery floss as follows: eyes, light blue, satin stitch; nose, pink, satin stitch; mouth, pink, stem stitch; sun rays, yellow, back stitch. If desired, lightly shade cheeks with pink Venus pencil.

3. Starting at underarm seam, stitch eyelet lace trim to cut sleeve edge, keeping eyelet binding even with raw sleeve edge. Open fold of single-fold white bias tape and pin fold line over eyelet binding edge with gathered eyelet, allowing ½" bias tape overlap at underarm seam. Stitch seam, fold bias tape to wrong side of sweatshirt sleeve and stitch bias tape casing on outer edge of bias tape, leaving open at underarm seam. Cut ¼" elastic to 6" piece and thread through bias tape casing. Stitch elastic ends together with ½" seam allowance and trim ends. Overlap, tuck and handstitch bias tape casing closed. Tie bow with hot pink mini-dot grosgrain ribbon, cutting ends in V. Tack bow to right side of casing stitching, opposite underarm seam. Repeat for other sleeve (see Diag. 3-1 in pattern section).

4. Cut out main appliqué scene as follows:

1 teddy bear head, 1 body, 2 feet: tan velour
1 teddy bear muzzle: tan with white mini-print
1 hat and shovel: pink print
1 sunsuit: white pastel floral print

1 pail and bird wing: light blue print
1 bird, 4 starfish: yellow and white floral print

5. Cut piece of lightweight iron-on interfacing slightly larger than appliqué scene and fuse to wrong side of sweatshirt front. This procedure stabilizes the sweatshirt knit from stretching while appliquéing. Be sure to use a ballpoint machine needle for best results.

6. Position and pin teddy bear head, body, sunsuit, and pail per placement drawing. Appliqué these pieces, using medium-width zigzag satin stitch. Make sure arms are lifted over sunsuit at bottom. Position, pin, and appliqué the rest of the design with medium-width zigzag satin stitch in this order: muzzle, hat, two feet, bird, bird's wing, shovel, and starfish.

7. Trim hat with scallop lace trim and tack small, hot pink mini-dot grosgrain ribbon bow at right side of hat. Cut out teddy bear eyes and nose from brown felt and glue in place with non-soluble tacky glue. Draw in mouth with water-soluble marking pen, and paint or embroider mouth in black. If desired, lightly shade cheeks and left inner ear with pink Venus pencil.

8. Cut two lace hearts and glue to shoulders of sunsuit. Draw a pail handle with water-soluble marking pen, then embroider with two strands of pink floss in stem stitch. Tie bow, using ¼"-wide white satin ribbon and tack to left side of pail handle. Glue pink nosegay flower just above bow. Embroider bird's beak with two strands pink embroidery floss in straight stitch and embroider bird's eye with two strands of light blue floss in french knot. Hand-topstitch lines indicated on starfish.

9. Tie bow, using remaining hot pink mini-dot grosgrain ribbon, cut ends in V and tack at lower left neckline.

BOY'S COVER-UP

- Cost of materials: $8.00
- Retail cost: $35.00

Materials
1 purchased aqua sweatshirt
6" of yellow knit ribbing
2 white bird buttons
1 package lightweight iron-on interfacing
Scraps of:
    tan velour
    white piqué
    bright yellow, hot pink, and bright aqua sailcloth
    tan and white mini-floral print
    black acrylic felt
3" of ¼"-wide aqua satin ribbon
Embroidery floss in bright aqua, hot pink, and yellow

Water-soluble marking pen
Non-soluble tacky glue
Pink Venus pencil
Matching threads

Directions

1. Cut off sleeves to short sleeve length. If you are unsure of amount to cut, a good rule of thumb is to fold sleeve in half and cut one inch above fold. On sizes 7 and up, you can cut two inches above fold.

2. Cut yellow ribbing into two pieces, 4″ by 6″. Seam 4″ sides together with ¼″ seam allowance to make tube. Fold ribbing to 2″ wide, with seam on inside; match seam to underarm sleeve seam with right sides together. Stretch ribbing to fit sleeve, pin; stitch, using ¼″ seam allowance. Zigzag stitch over raw edge of ribbing to encase seam. Repeat for other sleeve.

3. Back all scrap fabrics listed with lightweight iron-on interfacing. Cut out appliqué scene pieces:

1 each, cloud, sailor's cap, sailboat sail, and beach ball: white piqué
1 each, teddy bear head and teddy bear body: tan velour
1 teddy bear muzzle: tan and white mini-floral
1 each, sun, collar, and beach ball wedge: yellow sailcloth
1 each, sandbox, sailboat flag, and beach ball wedge: hot pink sailcloth
1 each, sailboat bottom, shovel, and beach ball wedge: bright aqua sailcloth

4. Cut a piece of lightweight iron-on interfacing, slightly larger than appliqué scene, and fuse to wrong side of sweatshirt front. This procedure stabilizes the sweatshirt knit so it does not stretch while appliquéing. Be sure to use a ballpoint sewing machine needle for best results.

5. Position, pin, and appliqué sun and cloud in upper lefthand sky. Draw sun face and sun rays, using water-soluble marking pen. Embroider sun face using two strands embroidery floss as follows: eyes, bright aqua, satin stitch; eyebrows, bright aqua, straight stitch; nose, hot pink, satin stitch; mouth, hot pink, stem stitch; sun rays, yellow, back stitch. If desired, lightly shade cheeks using pink Venus pencil.

6. Position and pin bear head, body, and pink sandbox per placement drawing. Appliqué above pieces using medium-width zigzag satin stitch. Make sure left arm is lifted over sandbox edge. Position, pin, and appliqué the rest of the appliqué with medium-width zigzag satin stitch in this order: bear's muzzle, sailor's cap, collar, shovel, white piqué beach ball, hot pink beach ball wedge, yellow beach ball wedge, bright aqua beach ball wedge, white piqué sail, bright aqua boat bottom, hot pink sailboat flag.

7. Cut out 2 eyes and nose from black acrylic felt; glue in place with non-soluble tacky glue. Stitch mouth, using black thread, in a single long stitch. Lightly

shade left inner ear and cheeks of face with pink Venus pencil. Draw shovel handle with water-soluble marking pen, then embroider handle using two strands of bright aqua embroidery floss in back stitch. Topstitch the following pieces in place, using straight machine stitch and aqua thread: sailboat mast, sailor's collar, and sailor's cap.

8. Stitch two white bird buttons in upper right sky. Tie knot in center of aqua ribbon and tack through knot to collar center (Diag. 3-2; see pattern section). Cut ribbon ends at an angle.

HOODED TEDDY BEAR TOWEL

Many of the exclusive boutique shops regularly stock hooded beach towels, but none with the twinkling appeal of the very special beach bear shown in Fig. 3-3. It's a charming cover-up that goes together in a jiffy. Also included is a simple adaptation for boys.

- Cost of materials: $14.00
- Retail Cost: $45.00

Materials

I yard top quality chocolate brown terrycloth
2 packages extra-wide light blue bias tape
⅛ yard tan terrycloth
½ yard 1"-wide gathered eyelet lace trim
½ yard medium-width pink rickrack
¼ yard 1"-wide hot pink taffeta picot ribbon
6" of ⅜"-wide teddy bear novelty ribbon
⅛ yard pink heart print fabric
Hot pink and black acrylic felt scraps
Matching threads

Directions

1. Cut chocolate brown terrycloth in 36" square. Round all four corners, using hood pattern outer edge as a guide. Cut hood and 4 ears from remaining chocolate brown terrycloth. Cut 2 inner ears from pink heart fabric and 1 muzzle from tan terrycloth. From black acrylic felt, cut 2 eyes, 1 nose, and 1 mouth. Cut two heart cheeks from hot pink acrylic felt.

2. Following placement drawing (Diag. 3-3), position, pin, and appliqué teddy face on hood, using wide-width zigzag satin stitch in the following order: eyes, muzzle, mouth, nose, and heart cheeks.

3. Add eyelet lace trim to hood edge under muzzle, matching binding edge to right side raw edge of hood. Fold under edge so eyelet binding does not show and stitch pink rickrack along edge. Tie bow, using hot pink picot taffeta ribbon, and tack under chin.

Fig. 3–3 Hooded Teddy
Bear Towel, Teddy Tote,
girl's and boy's thongs.

4. Stitch pink heart inner ears to main ear with medium-width zigzag satin stitch. Pin appliquéd ear and plain ear, right sides together, and stitch around ear with ¼" seam allowance, leaving flat side open per pattern. Repeat for other ear. Turn ears right side out and press. Pinch ears slightly in middle and baste to hood per pattern, appliquéd side facing down.

5. Baste hood to corner of towel. Starting at opposite end of towel, encase raw edge in extra-wide light blue bias tape. Stitch around entire perimeter of towel, overlapping bias tape with a new piece as necessary. Hand stitch ends, overlapping and tucking them under for a finished look.

6. Tack ears back to bias tape so they stand up. Tie bow, using ⅜"-wide teddy bear novelty ribbon and tack to bottom of fold in left ear.

Fig. 3–4 Bikini and swim trunks.

Boy's Towel Adaptations

• Line inner ears with light blue heart fabric instead of pink heart print fabric.
• Omit eyelet trim around edge of hood and trim with white jumbo rickrack instead.
• Tie 1"-wide light blue stripe grosgrain ribbon into bow and tack under chin (instead of pink ribbon).

A BEAR-Y SPECIAL BIKINI

The bikini shown in Fig. 3-4 can be made in the morning and worn to the pool in the afternoon. The bikini bottoms are made using a purchased bloomer pattern with a few adaptations. Bikini top will fit 2- to 6-year olds. Enlarge the pattern given by 25% for older girls.

■ Cost of materials: $10.00
■ Retail cost: $25.00

Materials
Purchased bloomer pattern
½ yard medium brown poplin

4″ square tan poplin
2 yards 2″-wide double-edge ruffled eyelet
3 yards ⅜″-wide hot pink mini-dot grosgrain ribbon
1 yard 1″-wide gathered eyelet lace trim
1 yard single-fold white bias tape
½ yard ¼″-wide elastic
½ yard ½″-wide elastic
4″ by 8″ piece Thermolam batting
Scraps of black and hot pink acrylic felt
4 ¼″ black buttons
2″ square of pink poplin
Hot pink and black acrylic paint
Matching threads

Directions

1. Stitch hot pink mini-dot ribbon down center of double-edge ruffled eyelet lace. Save additional yard of pink ribbon for bows. Cut ribbon-trimmed eyelet into four 18″ pieces.

2. Cut 4 bear heads (2 in reverse) from brown poplin, two muzzles from tan poplin, 4 hearts from pink acrylic felt, and 2 noses from black acrylic felt.

3. Back two bear heads with lightweight iron-on interfacing. Using medium-width satin stitch, appliqué muzzle to bear face, nose to muzzle, and heart cheeks to muzzle as indicated on pattern. Repeat for second bear.

4. Cut Thermolam batting into two 4″-square pieces. Layer with batting on bottom, appliquéd bear head right-side-up on batting, and plain bear head right-side-down. Pin and stitch around bear head using ¼″ seam allowance, leaving 2-inch opening at bottom of head. Trim away excess batting and clip curves. Turn and blind stitch closed.

5. Topstitch ears and sew on button eyes, following pattern for placement. Paint inner ears, using dry brush and pink acrylic paint. Paint mouth, using black acrylic paint. Repeat for second bear.

6. Make two small and two medium-size bows from hot pink mini-dot ribbon. Tack medium-size bows under chin and small bows at outer ears, per photo. Tack heads together at center of inner face edges.

7. Hem all ends of eyelet-ribbon trim and hand sew to sides and mid-outer-edge of ears of bear heads for ties. Set completed top aside.

8. Using purchased bloomer pattern, fold down waistband 2½″ and cut out bikini bottoms, per pattern instructions. Cut pink heart from pink poplin and pin to middle of left side of front. Appliqué heart in place, using medium-width zigzag satin stitch.

9. Fold, press, and stitch waistband casing, following bloomer pattern directions.

10. Edge leg openings with eyelet lace and use bias tape to form casing for elastic. Complete, following pattern directions.

11. Tie two medium-size bows, using hot pink mini-dot ribbon; tack to leg openings just above eyelet trim on sides.

TEDDY TRUNKS

Using purchased pattern for shorts, with elastic casing waist, these swim trunks can also be used for shorts (Fig. 3-4). When making them for a toddler, purchase an inexpensive pair of terry training pants and tack its waistband under waistband casing of trunks, then stitch waistband casing.

- Cost of materials: $4.75
- Retail cost: $12.00

Materials

Purchased pattern for simple elastic-waist shorts
½ yard medium brown poplin
⅛ yard bright aqua poplin
Scraps of:
    tan mini-dot fabric
    black acrylic felt
    jumbo white rickrack
    ⅜"-wide teddy bear novelty ribbon
    lightweight iron-on interfacing
Pink and black acrylic paints
Matching threads

Directions

1. Following purchased pattern instructions, cut out trunks. Back scraps of medium-brown poplin and tan mini-dot fabric with lightweight iron-on interfacing. Cut two pockets from bright aqua poplin, 1 teddy face from medium brown poplin, 1 muzzle from tan mini-dot fabric, and 1 nose from black acrylic felt.

2. Center teddy head appliqué on pocket; appliqué in place, using medium-width zigzag satin stitch. Appliqué muzzle and nose per pattern placement, using narrow zigzag stitch. Using dry brush, paint inner ear of bear with pink acrylic paint. Paint eyes and mouth, using black acrylic paint. Stitch white jumbo rickrack across top of pocket. With right sides together, stitch around perimeter of pocket with ¼" seam allowance, leaving open at pocket bottom for turning. Clip corners, turn, press, and hand stitch closed.

3. Position pocket on left front side of shorts and outline stitch around pocket, leaving top open. Make a bow from teddy bear ribbon and tack at chin of bear.

4. Finish trunks according to pattern instructions.

46

TRIMMED THONGS

The thongs shown in Fig. 3-3 will put snap in your tot's step. Bits of ribbon and trim turn ordinary flip-flops into fancy footwear. Even teens have a hard time resisting the appeal of funky footwear!

Girl's Thongs

- Cost of materials: $2.50
- Retail cost: $12.00

Materials

1 pair purchased thongs (usually on sale for $.69 to $.99)
1½ to 2 yards 1"-wide pink gingham taffeta ribbon (depending on thong size)
1 can Scotchguard spray
1 stick Krazy Glue

Directions

1. Cut pink gingham ribbon into two 9" and two 18" pieces for sizes up to age 5. (Cut two 9" ribbons and cut remaining ribbon in half for larger sizes.) Saturate ribbon thoroughly with Scotchguard spray and let dry overnight.

2. Tie 9" ribbon pieces into bows, cutting ends in V shape, and set aside.

3. Read all instructions on package of Krazy Glue. Starting at one end of thong cut in sole, wedge end of 18" ribbon piece in hole and glue. Carefully wrap ribbon around thong strap, placing dot of Krazy Glue under ribbon at each wrap-around. Wrap ribbon so it just slightly overlaps. At center (separating big and little toes), wrap ribbon over, under, and around, dotting thong with glue at each step. Wrap ribbon around remaining strap, dotting with glue as you go. Wedge end of ribbon into sole hole and glue securely.

4. Glue bow in center of Y that separates toes. Repeat for other thong.

Boy's Teddy Thongs

- Cost of materials: $5.00
- Retail cost: $15.00

Materials

1 pair purchased thongs
1 yard 1"-wide light blue mini-dot grosgrain ribbon
¼ yard ⅜"-wide teddy bear novelty ribbon
¼ yard ⅛"-wide light blue satin ribbon
⅛ yard tan velour
Scraps of brown and black acrylic felt
4–6mm brown animal eyes
Polyfil stuffing

Black fine-line Sharpie marker
Pink Venus pencil
Hot glue gun and glue sticks
1 can Scotchguard
1 stick Krazy Glue
Matching threads

Directions

1. Cut light blue mini-dot grosgrain ribbon into two 18" pieces. (More ribbon may be needed for larger sizes.) Saturate ribbon thoroughly with Scotchguard spray and let dry overnight.

2. Wrap and glue ribbon around straps, following directions in Step 3 of Girl's Thongs.

3. To make bear heads, trace 2 bear faces on wrong side of velour. With right sides together, stitch on traced line. Cut out faces, leaving 1/8" seam allowance. Cut a slit in back of head, being careful not to cut through more than one layer, and turn right-side-out. Stuff and stitch closed. Take a little tuck stitch under each inner ear and pull thread to indent ear a little. Lightly shade inner ear, using pink Venus pencil.

4. Cut muzzle from brown felt and hand stitch, running stitch around outer edge of muzzle. Put tiny amount of polyfil stuffing in center of muzzle and pull stitching tightly. Knot securely. Glue muzzle to face, following photo (Fig. 3-3). Cut out nose from black felt and glue in place. Stitch eyes per pattern, pulling tightly to indent area a little. Glue brown animal eyes in eye indentations. Using black Sharpie fine-line marker, draw in eyelashes and smiling mouth. Lightly shade cheeks, using pink Venus pencil. If desired, lightly shade inner ears with pink Venus pencil also.

5. Tie bow from 1/8" light blue satin ribbon and glue to bottom of right ear. Tie bow using 3/8"-wide teddy bear novelty ribbon and glue under chin. Using Krazy Glue stick, glue bear head to Y that separates toes of thong. Repeat for other thong.

Funky Feet Thongs

- Cost of materials: $5.00
- Retail Cost: $12.50

Materials

1 pair purchased thongs
1½ yards 1"-wide lavender gingham taffeta ribbon
½ yard each of lavender, pink, and white 6"-wide nylon net
6 novelty buttons in pastel colors
Invisible nylon thread

Directions

1. Cut lavender gingham ribbon in half and saturate thoroughly with Scotchguard spray. Let dry overnight.

2. Wrap and glue ribbon on sandal straps with Krazy Glue, following directions in Step 3 under Girl's Thongs.

3. Cut nylon net into 3"-wide strips. Layer lavender, pink, and white net; gather down center lengthwise with invisible nylon thread and knot securely. Do not cut thread, but string on 3 novelty buttons. Knot securely and cut thread. Glue "funky" net flower to center of Y that separates toes, using Krazy Glue. Repeat for other thong.

TEDDY BEAR SHIRT AND SHORT SET

This outfit is shown in the color section.

- Cost of materials: $9.50
- Retail cost: $35.00

Materials

1 purchased aqua cotton knit polo shirt
2 teddy bear buttons
Purchased pattern for simple shorts with elastic casing waist
½ yard aqua Trigger
½ yard ½"-wide white elastic
    (or purchased pair of aqua shorts)
Scraps of:
    medium brown poplin
    tan with white mini-floral print
    hot pink acrylic felt
    lightweight iron-on interfacing
6" of ⅜"-wide teddy bear novelty ribbon
Black acrylic paint
Water-soluble marking pen
Pink Venus pencil
Matching threads

Directions

1. Remove original shirt buttons and set aside. Replace buttons with teddy bear buttons, enlarging buttonholes if needed.

2. Back scraps of medium brown poplin and tan with white mini-floral print fabrics with lightweight iron-on interfacing. Cut out teddy bear face from medium brown poplin and muzzle from tan and white mini-floral print. Cut two tiny heart cheeks from hot pink acrylic felt.

3. Cut piece of lightweight iron-on interfacing slightly larger than teddy bear face. Fuse interfacing to wrong side at upper right side of shirt front. This procedure stabilizes knit fabric to prevent stretching while appliquéing. Be sure to use ballpoint sewing machine needle for best results.

4. Position, pin, and appliqué teddy bear face to shirt front as shown in color section, using medium-width zigzag satin stitch. Position, pin, and appliqué muzzle to teddy face with narrow zigzag satin stitch.

5. With water-soluble marking pen, draw eyes, nose, and mouth per pattern. Using black acrylic paint, hand paint eyes, nose, and mouth. Shade inner ears with pink Venus pencil. Tack hot pink felt heart cheeks to sides of muzzle, as indicated on pattern.

6. Tie ⅜"-wide teddy bear novelty ribbon into bow and tack at chin. Set finished shirt aside.

7. If using purchased shorts, cut pawprint appliqué pieces from medium brown poplin backed with lightweight iron-on interfacing. Per photograph, position, pin, and appliqué pawprint to right front side of shorts, using medium-width zigzag satin stitch. Press lightly.

8. If making shorts, cut out from aqua Trigger according to pattern instructions. Position, pin, and appliqué teddy bear pawprint to right front side of shorts, using medium-width zigzag satin stitch. Press lightly. Complete shorts per purchased pattern instructions.

Variations on a Theme

• Trim purchased shirts and shorts with appliqués, using a variety of summer theme ideas. Some suggestions:

ON SHIRT	ON SHORTS
Mouse	Swiss cheese
Bunny	Carrot
Puppy	Bone
Daisy	Bumblebee

• Flip through your children's coloring books for a wealth of ideas for simple drawings to use as appliqué designs that can mirror their special interests.

TEDDY BEAR TOTE

This versatile tote is shown in Fig. 3-3.

- Cost of materials: $5.00
- Retail cost: $12.50

Materials
⅓ yard hot pink canvas
¼ yard bright yellow canvas
1⅛ yards 1"-wide gathered eyelet lace trim

2 yards 1"-wide aqua webbing
15" of apple green jumbo rickrack
6" of ⅜"-wide hot pink mini-dot grosgrain ribbon
Scraps of:
    medium brown poplin
    tan with white mini-floral print
    lightweight iron-on interfacing
    hot pink acrylic felt
Black acrylic paint
Pink Venus pencil
Matching threads

Directions
    1. Cut hot pink canvas into rectangle, 12" wide × 22" long. Cut yellow canvas rectangle, 7" wide × 13" long.
    2. Stitch eyelet lace to 7" side of yellow canvas piece, sewing eyelet binding along fabric edge. Fold under eyelet binding ¼", so gathered eyelet shows at edge of yellow pocket; press. Stitch apple green jumbo rickrack across eyelet-trimmed edge. Repeat for other 7" side.
    3. Fold yellow canvas right-side-out, matching eyelet lace ends; press.
    4. Back medium brown poplin, and tan with white mini-floral print, with lightweight iron-on interfacing. Cut out teddy bear face from medium-brown poplin and muzzle from tan print. Center teddy bear face on folded yellow pocket. Unfold pocket and pin bear face. Appliqué face using medium-width zigzag satin stitch. Position, pin, and appliqué muzzle, using narrow zigzag satin stitch. With water-soluble marking pen, draw eyes, nose, and mouth per pattern. Paint features, using black acrylic paint. Shade ears with pink Venus pencil. Cut two heart cheeks from hot pink acrylic felt and tack in place. Tie bow with hot pink mini-dot grosgrain ribbon and cut ends in V shape. Tack bow under bear chin.
    5. Fold short ends of hot pink canvas together and press. Using foldlines on pink canvas and yellow pocket as a guide, center yellow pocket piece across pink tote. Baste long edges of pocket to tote with ⅛" seam allowance.
    6. Stitch eyelet lace trim along 12" edge of pink canvas, with eyelet binding along fabric edge. Fold under eyelet binding ¼" so gathered eyelet shows at edge, and press. Topstitch ⅛" from fold. Repeat for other 12" side.
    7. Pin to mark webbing at 1 yard. Center webbing with ends overlapping on center foldline ½" and overlapping pocket edge ¼". Center the pin mark on fold line of other side of pocket edge ¼". See Diag. 3-4. Baste webbing along length of tote. Zigzag stitch along edge of webbing on both sides to top of tote. Zigzag stitch across top of webbing at tote top. Repeat for other side of pocket.
    8. With right sides together, stitch side seams with ¼" seam allowance. Finish seam edge by zigzag stitching over raw seam edge. Turn right-side-out and press.

Summer Variations

- Any variety of colors can be used for the basic tote. Also, you can use other appliqués in this book or devise your own designs.
- The tote or garments in this chapter can be personalized using the alphabet provided in Winter Wonderland, Chapter 5. The possibilities are endless.
- Use lamb appliqué in Chapter 2 for your summer theme. Coordinate with 3-D daisy appliqué in hot pastel colors (found in the fall sweater section, Chapter 4).
- Vary animal faces used to trim thongs, then carry that theme throughout summer ensemble.
- Use teddy appliqué on sundresses, purchased swimwear, pajamas, or even rainwear. Using acrylic paints, paint teddy motif on umbrella, slicker, and rainboots. After paint has dried 24 hours, seal with clear polyurethane varnish. Do not use polyurethane spray unless you are sure propellants won't damage vinyl.

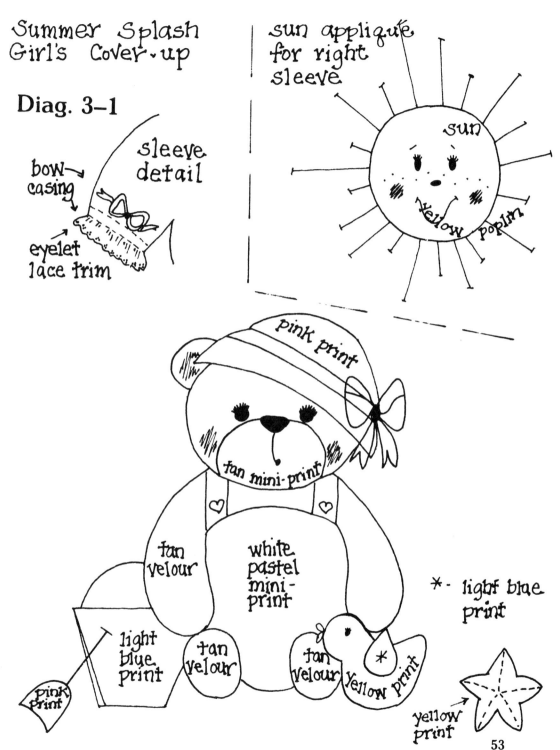

Summer Splash
Girl's Cover-up

Diag. 3-1

bow
casing

eyelet
lace trim

sleeve
detail

sun applique
for right
sleeve

sun

yellow poplin

pink print

tan mini-print

tan
velour

white
pastel
mini-
print

light
blue
print

tan
velour

tan
velour

yellow print

* - light blue
print

Pink
Print

yellow
print

53

Girl's cover-up pattern placement guide

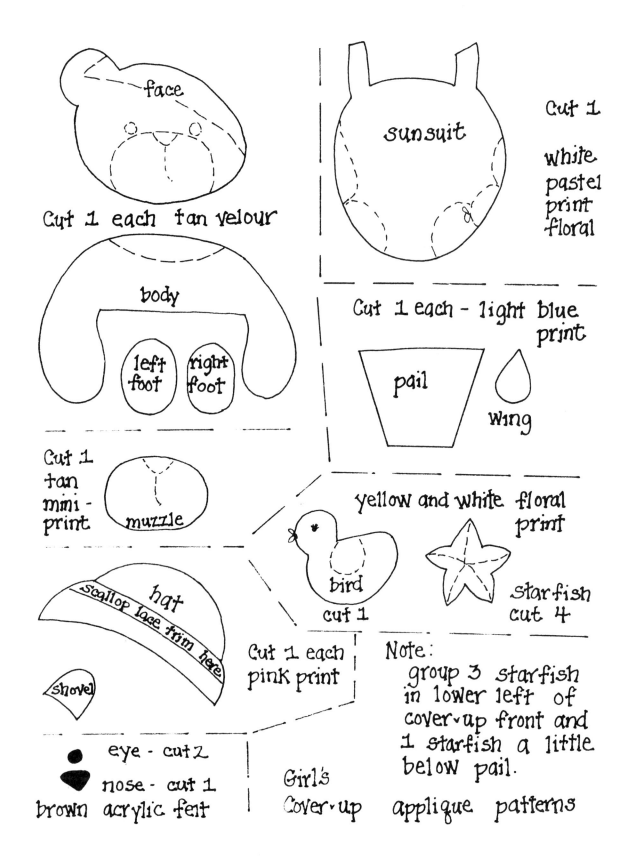

face

Cut 1 each tan velour

body

left foot

right foot

Cut 1 tan mini-print

muzzle

hat

scallop lace trim here

shovel

eye - cut 2

nose - cut 1

brown acrylic felt

Girl's Cover-up

Cut 1 each pink print

sunsuit

Cut 1

white pastel print floral

Cut 1 each - light blue print

pail

wing

yellow and white floral print

bird cut 1

starfish cut 4

Note:
  group 3 starfish in lower left of cover-up front and 1 starfish a little below pail.

applique patterns

Summer Splash * Boy's Cover-up Pattern Placement

X - white bird buttons

cloud
white piqué

sun -
yellow
sailcloth

X

X

tv - tan velour
wp - white piqué
hp - hot pink sailcloth
ys - yellow sailcloth
as - bright aqua sailcloth
tmf - tan mini-floral

sailor's cap
wp
head
tv
tmf
muzzle
sailor's collar
ys
body tv
hp

ys wp
wp hp
as wp
beach ball
as
shovel

sandbox-
hot pink
sailcloth

wp
ys

Summer Splash Boy's Cover-up

head

sail

cloud

body

sailor's cap

beach ball

Cut 1 each - tan velour

Cut 1 each - white piqué

muzzle

sandbox

flag

beach ball wedge

cut 1 - tan mini-floral

cut 1 each - hot pink sailcloth

cut 1 each - yellow sailcloth

sun

boat bottom

←shovel

beach ball wedge →

cut 1 each bright aqua sailcloth

sailor's collar

↙ribbon
Knot at "x"
of sailor's collar

Diag. 3-2

beach ball ←wedge

● eye - cut 2
♥ nose - cut 1
black acrylic felt

Appliqué pattern pieces

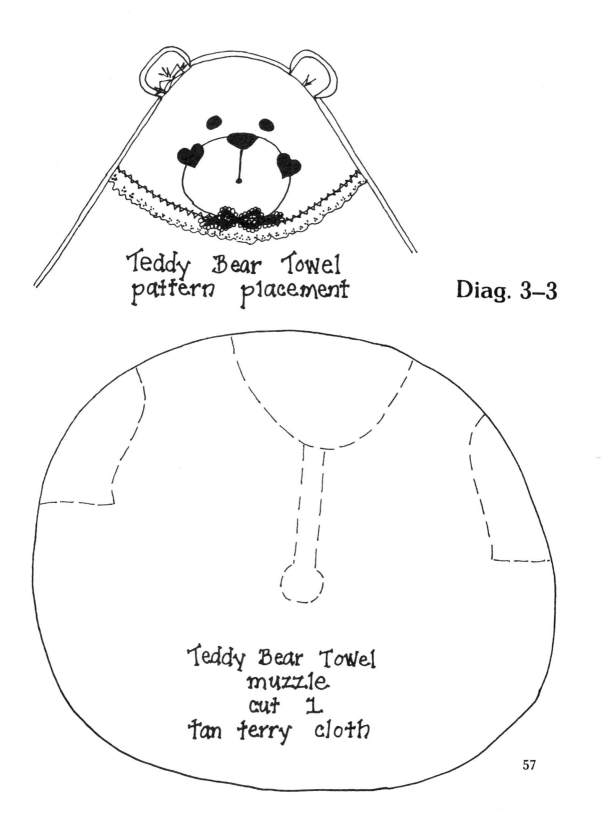

Teddy Bear Towel
pattern placement

Diag. 3-3

Teddy Bear Towel
muzzle
cut 1
tan terry cloth

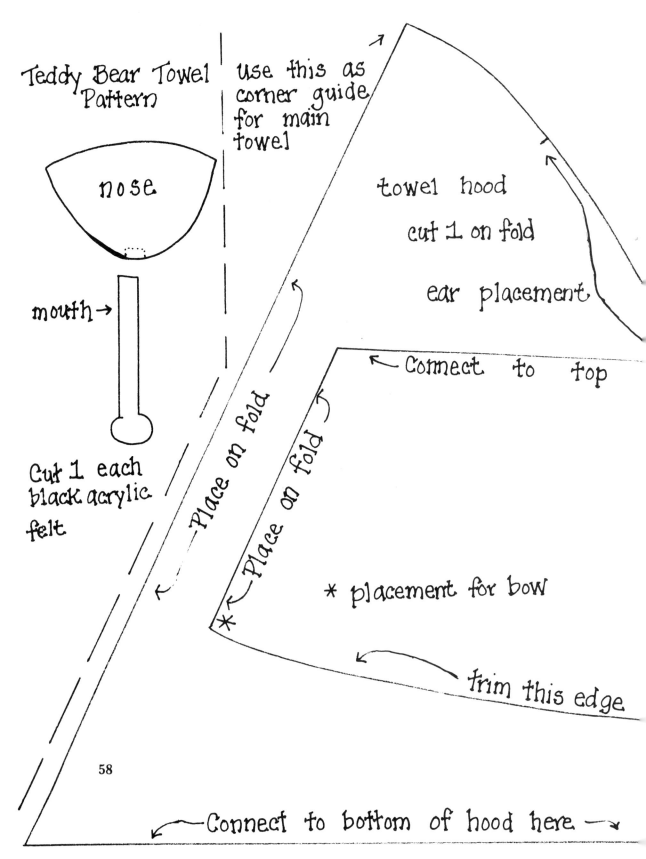

Teddy Bear Towel Pattern

nose

mouth →

Cut 1 each black acrylic felt

use this as corner guide for main towel

Place on fold

towel hood

cut 1 on fold

ear placement

Place on fold

Place on fold

Connect to top

* placement for bow

*

trim this edge

58

Connect to bottom of hood here.

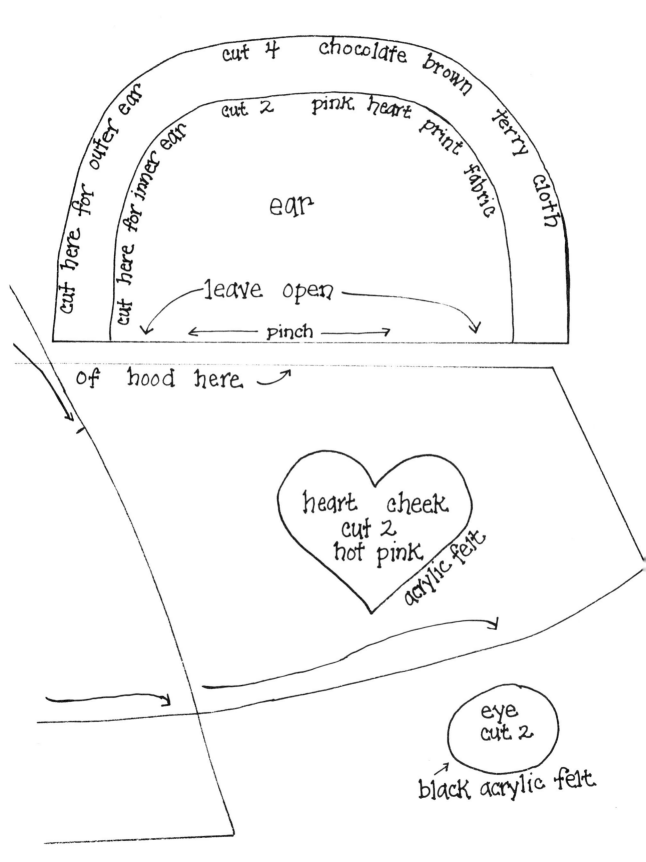

cut 4   chocolate brown terry cloth

cut here for outer ear

cut here for inner ear   cut 2   pink heart print fabric

ear

leave open

← pinch →

of hood here.

heart cheek
cut 2
hot pink
acrylic felt

eye
cut 2

black acrylic felt

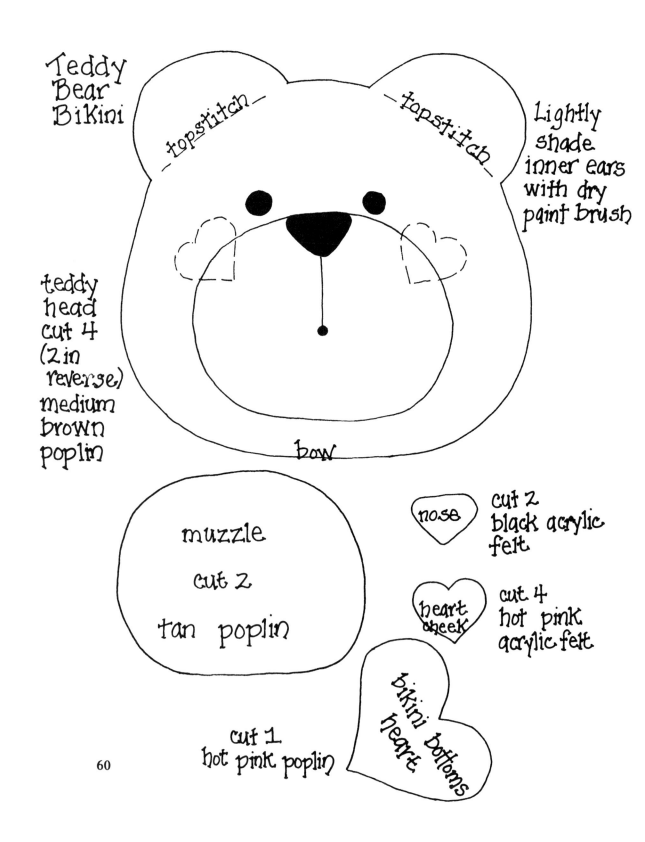

Teddy Bear Bikini

topstitch   topstitch

Lightly shade inner ears with dry paint brush

teddy head cut 4 (2 in reverse) medium brown poplin

bow

muzzle

cut 2

tan poplin

nose — cut 2 black acrylic felt

heart cheek — cut 4 hot pink acrylic felt

bikini bottoms heart

cut 1 hot pink poplin

60

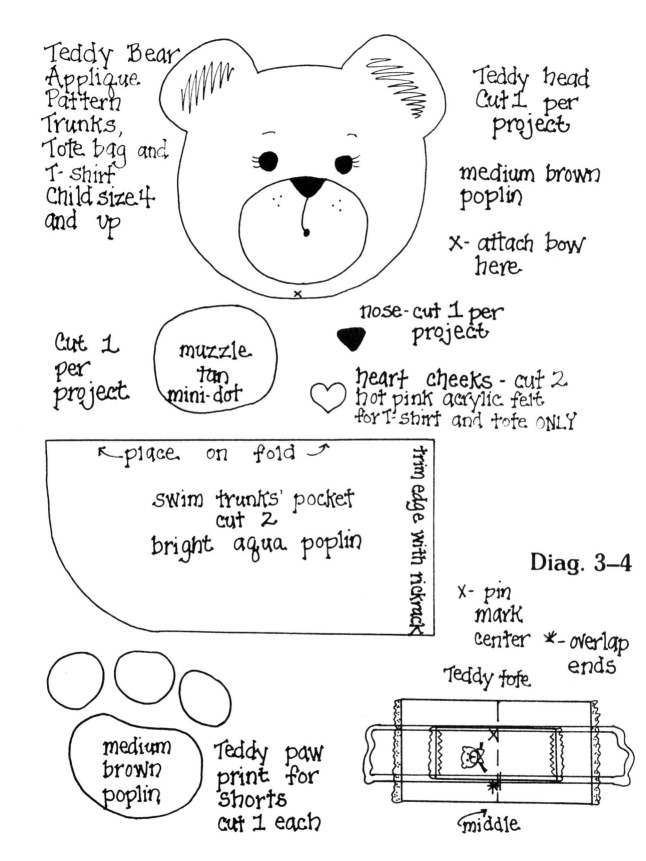

Teddy Bear
Applique
Pattern
Trunks,
Tote bag and
T-shirt
Child size 4
and up

Teddy head
Cut 1 per
project

medium brown
poplin

X- attach bow
here

Cut 1
per
project

muzzle
tan
mini-dot

nose-cut 1 per
project

heart cheeks - cut 2
hot pink acrylic felt
for T-shirt and tote ONLY

← place on fold →

swim trunks' pocket
cut 2
bright aqua poplin

trim edge with rickrack

Diag. 3-4

X- pin
mark
center ✳- overlap
ends

Teddy tote

medium
brown
poplin

Teddy paw
print for
Shorts
cut 1 each

middle

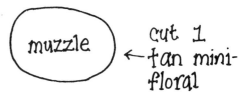

muzzle ← cut 1 tan mini-floral

♡ ← heart cheeks cut 2 hot pink acrylic felt

Teddy bear t-shirt appliqué for infants through toddler size 4

muzzle — cut 2 brown acrylic felt

♡ ← nose cut 2 black acrylic felt

Teddy Bear Thongs

trace around bear head per instructions

* attach bow here

CHAPTER 4

Americana Autumn:
Back to School

Children of all ages look forward to old friendships, new lunchboxes, and a chance to wear their wonderful new wardrobes as back-to-school days loom ever closer. The bright primary colors of crayons enhance the Animal Crackers theme, featuring bib jumper, sweater and pants set, and versatile vest. An assortment of Snazzy Sweaters becomes the perfect match for the crisp breezes of Fall.

ANIMAL CRACKERS VEST

Don't let the elaborate look of the vest (Figs. 4-1 and 4-2) fool you—it's much easier to make than it appears. This project is an excellent example of dividing the completed project into easy-to-do parts.

The vest uses the front and back pieces of the Springtime Splendor jacket pattern in Chapter 2, or you may substitute a purchased vest pattern. The pattern pieces are divided into three equal parts horizontally, appliquéd with animals, assembled, and quilted. Finishing touches of bows, buttons, and bells make this vest an instant favorite. The vest shown was made in a child's size 6, but the appliqués may be arranged to accommodate up to a size 12.

- Cost of materials: $13.00
- Retail cost: $65.00

Materials

Purchased simple vest pattern *or* front and back patterns from Springtime
    Splendor jacket
⅓ yard red Trigger
⅓ yard green Trigger
⅓ yard royal blue Trigger
1 yard green dot fabric
1 yard Thermolam batting
12″ red separating zipper
    (for child's size 6; check pattern for amounts and sizes needed)
12″ extra-wide royal blue bias tape
Lightweight iron-on interfacing

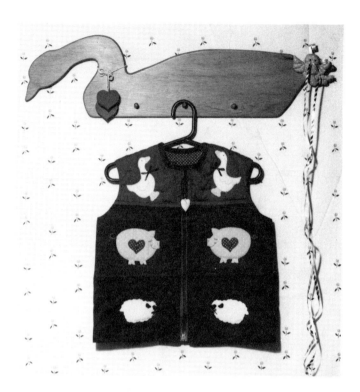

Fig. 4–1 Animal Crackers
vest.

Scraps of:
   white piqué
   bright yellow Trigger
   pink heart fabric
   black mini-dot fabric
   yellow multicolored floral print
   tan and white mini-floral print
   brown mini-dot fabric
   red mini-dot fabric
   ⅛″-wide royal blue satin ribbon
   ⅛″-wide red satin ribbon
   ⅛″-wide hot pink satin ribbon
3 red ⅜″ heart buttons
2 tiny ¼″ brass bells
1 small cow bell
Embroidery floss in light blue, light pink, hot pink, and brown
1 white heart zipper pull for girl or 1 whistle zipper pull for boy
Water-soluble marking pen
Matching threads

Fig. 4–2 Back of vest.

Directions

1. Use purchased vest pattern or the front and back pieces from the Spring-time Splendor jacket. To make pattern, trace two front pieces and one back piece on brown paper: cut-up grocery bags are good for this. Square off front bottom piece if necessary (Diag. 4-1). Cut out pieces and tape side seams together, over-lapping seam allowances. Using a yardstick, measure length of center back. Divide this measurement by three and mark pattern to be divided into three equal parts horizontally. Use a yardstick to help draw dividing lines across brown paper pattern with bright magic marker. Fold pattern in half vertically at center back and check to see that all dividing lines match evenly at front. Adjust as necessary.

2. Cut brown paper pattern on dividing lines. You will have three top sections: A, left front top; B, right front top; and C, back top. You'll have one middle section, D, with scoops for armholes; and one bottom section, E, a single long strip (Diag. 4-2).

3. Add ¼″ seam allowance to bottom of pieces A, B, and C; ¼″ seam allowance to top and bottom of D, and ¼″ seam allowance to top of E (Diag. 4-3). Cut pieces A, B, and C from red Trigger, piece D from green Trigger, and piece E from royal blue Trigger.

4. To appliqué top section pieces A, B, and C, back the white piqué, yellow

Trigger, and yellow multicolored floral print fabric with lightweight iron-on interfacing. Cut out appliqué pieces as follows:

3 goose bodies: white piqué
3 goose beaks and 3 goose feet: yellow Trigger
2 hearts: yellow floral print

Please note that some pieces should be *cut in reverse,* as indicated on the pattern piece; also see Diag. 4-4 for direction each appliqué faces.

5. Fold piece C in half vertically to determine center back. Position and pin goose body at center back with beak and feet tucked in, per pattern. Mark eye, wing, and feet topstitching details with water-soluble marking pen. Using medium-width zigzag satin stitch, appliqué body, beak, and feet, using bright yellow thread. Zigzag satin stitch wing and feet details. Embroider eye with two strands of light blue embroidery floss, using satin stitch. Position and pin yellow print hearts on each side of goose with hearts slightly lying on their sides and bottom points toward goose. Appliqué hearts with medium-width zigzag satin stitch. Tie tiny bow, using ⅛"-wide royal blue satin ribbon, and tack at bottom of goose's neck. Press piece and set aside.

6. Using piece A, position and pin goose body at an angle so goose is facing up and in toward center front (see photograph, Fig. 4-1). Following appliqué instructions for goose in step 5, appliqué and trim goose. Using piece B, *reverse* position of goose. Pin and position goose to face front piece A at center front. It is easier if you place completed piece A on left and piece B on right. Maneuver appliqués until you get an exact mirror image, then pin. Appliqué and trim goose per instructions in step 5. Press both pieces A and B and set aside.

7. To appliqué middle section D, back white piqué, brown mini-dot fabric, tan and white mini-floral print, pink heart print, and green dot scraps with lightweight iron-on interfacing. Cut out appliqué pieces as follows:

1 cow body: brown mini-dot fabric
1 cow head: tan and white mini-floral print
1 cow mouth and 1 hind spot: white piqué
1 cow udder and 2 pigs: pink heart print
2 small hearts: green dot

Please note that some pieces must be cut in reverse: follow instructions on pattern pieces.

8. Fold piece D in half vertically to determine center back. Position and pin cow body at center back, tucking in udder on right lower side of cow, per pattern. Appliqué cow body and udder using medium-width zigzag satin stitch. Position and pin cow head and mouth at a jaunty angle and appliqué, using narrow zigzag satin stitch. Position, pin, and appliqué cow hind spot per pattern, using medium-width zigzag satin stitch. Using water-soluble marking pen, draw in eyes, nose,

mouth, and tail. Using two strands of embroidery floss, embroider features: eyes, brown, satin stitch; nose, light pink, satin stitch; mouth, hot pink, working smile in back stitch, and hearts in satin stitch; tail, brown, back stitch. Press.

9. Fold piece D so front sides meet at center front and armholes are evenly matched; press lightly. Position and pin pig bodies so they are centered on each front side, facing one another. Appliqué pigs with medium-width zigzag satin stitch. Pin green dot hearts to center of pig bodies and appliqué, using narrow zigzag satin stitch. Press. Using water-soluble marking pen, draw in eyes, nose, mouth, and tail. Using two strands of floss, embroider features: eyes, light blue, back stitch; nose, hot pink, lazy daisy stitch; mouth, hot pink, working smile in back stitch and heart in satin stitch; tail, hot pink, back stitch. Sew red heart buttons to center of green dot hearts. Press and set aside.

10. To appliqué lower section E, back white piqué, black mini-dot fabric, and red fabric scraps with lightweight iron-on interfacing. Cut out appliqué pieces as follows:

    3 lamb bodies: white piqué
    3 lamb faces, 3 lamb ears, 3 pair front legs, and 3 pair back legs: black mini-dot fabric
    2 hearts: red mini-dot fabric

Please note that some pieces are cut in reverse: follow directions on the pattern pieces.

11. Fold piece E in half vertically to determine center back. Position and pin lamb body at center back with face, front legs, and back legs tucked under white piqué body. Using medium-width zigzag satin stitch, appliqué around lamb body. With narrow zigzag satin stitch, appliqué face, front legs, and back legs. Position and appliqué ear. Embroider light blue eye on lamb face, using two strands of light blue embroidery floss in satin stitch or french knot. Sew red heart button under lamb's head.

12. Fold piece E so front sides meet at center front and lightly press, Position and pin lamb bodies so they are centered on each front side, facing each other. Appliqué lambs, per instructions in step 11. Position, pin, and appliqué red mini-dot hearts on each side of center lamb, one inch from side folds, with medium-width zigzag satin stitch. Press.

13. To assemble vest, pin piece D bottom to piece E top with right sides together. Check to be sure center lamb is directly under cow. Stitch seam, using ¼" seam allowance; press seam open. Pin piece C over center back section of vest, lining up armholes on each side and checking that goose is directly over cow. Stitch seam, using ¼" seam allowance; press seam open. Pin front side pieces A and B over pigs of section D, lining up armholes and checking to see that each goose is directly over pig. Stitch seam, using ¼" seam allowance; press open. Repeat for other front side. Trim any uneven perimeters and press vest as a whole.

14. Using assembled vest as a pattern, place appliquéd vest right-side-down on green dot lining fabric facing right-side-up. Pin and cut out green dot lining piece. Use green dot lining as pattern and cut 1 vest from Thermolam batting.

15. Separate zipper and baste each zipper side to front side of vest. Be sure to baste each side exactly the same way, so zipper will match up perfectly. Layer pieces as follows: batting on bottom, green dot lining facing right-side-up, then appliquéd vest facing right-side-down. Smooth layers carefully and pin sides, bottom, and armholes. Do not pin neckline. Starting at top of right side, seam right side, bottom, and up the left side, using ⅝" seam allowance. Stitch armhole seams, using ⅝" seam allowance. Clip curves and corners and trim seams to ¼". Turn right-side-out and press. Check to be sure zipper matches perfectly.

16. Pin shoulder seams with right sides together, matching lining and top seams; stitch seams, using ⅝" seam allowance. Trim seams to ¼" and press.

17. Trim neckline so all edges are even. Encase neckline with royal blue extra-wide bias tape and blind stitch hem ends.

18. To quilt vest, hand baste per Diag. 4-5. Please note that vest can be entirely machine quilted or entirely hand quilted. For the vest shown, I used machine quilting around main pieces and hand quilting around appliquéd animals and hearts.

Using green thread, machine quilt by topstitching top section from left armhole, ¼" above seam, to zipper, ¼" up to neckline, ⅛" around neckline, ¼" down zipper and ¼" across to other armhole. On back, topstitch ¼" above back seam.

Using royal blue thread, machine quilt by topstitching middle section ¼" below top section seam across back. Topstitch ¼" around green piece from underarm to zipper, to bottom of zipper, to top of piece to armhole.

Using royal blue thread, machine quilt by topstitching bottom section ¼" around perimeter.

Hand quilt around animals and hearts, pulling quilting thread slightly to give appliquéd pieces a little puff.

Remove basting stitches.

19. Sew small brass bells under lamb heads on vest front. Tie two tiny bows from ⅛" red satin ribbon and tack above bells. Sew cowbell just under cow's mouth. Tie tiny bow, using ⅛"-wide hot pink satin ribbon, and tack above cowbell. Clip on white heart zipper pull.

Variations on a Theme

- If making vest for a boy, substitute stars for hearts and use whistle zipper pull instead of heart.
- Make vest in pastel colors for Spring. Substitute basket appliqué for cow appliqué in middle section of back. Substitute bunny appliqué for pig in front middle section.
- For a sports-minded girl or boy, substitute appliqués of sports equipment such

as bats, balls, mitts, footballs, helmets, tennis rackets, and sneakers. Use special school or team colors for the main section pieces.

- If time is of the essence, cut out various section pieces from different plaids, assemble, and outline quilt. Add quilting to main pieces in shapes of hearts or stars, providing a bright, preppy look in a minimum of time.
- Use the main idea of dividing a vest into sections to make a rainbow vest in a jiffy. Purchase ⅛ yard each of Trigger in rainbow colors: red, hot pink, light pink, yellow, lime green, grass green, royal blue, and purple. Cut fabrics into 3″ strips and seam in rainbow order, using ¼″ seam allowance. Press seams open and cut out vest from pattern made in Step 1. Cut lining and batting from same pattern. Complete per instructions for vest and outline quilt ¼″ from each seam or, for a quick method, stitch-in-the-ditch.

ANIMAL CRACKERS JUMPER

Choose a simple purchased jumper pattern with a rounded bib top, shoulder straps, and gathered skirt. The jumper shown in Fig. 4-3 has contrasting bias binding around bib and side ties; however, these can be added to plain bib jumper pattern.

- Cost of materials: $12.00
- Retail cost: $35.00

Materials

1 purchased jumper pattern with rounded bib top and gathered skirt
⅝ yard red Trigger
¼ yard red Trigger
2 packages kelly green extra-wide bias tape
   (for child's size 6; check pattern instructions for amounts)
1½ yards jumbo kelly green rickrack
2 yellow ⅝″ sun buttons
2 red ⅝″ heart buttons
2 tiny ¼″ brass bells
Lightweight iron-on interfacing
Scraps of:
   white piqué
   bright yellow Trigger
   pink heart fabric
   green dot fabric
   red mini-dot fabric
   black mini-dot fabric
   ⅛″-wide royal blue satin ribbon
   ⅛″-wide red satin ribbon
Embroidery floss in light blue and hot pink

Water-soluble marking pen
Matching threads

Directions

　1. Trace skirt pattern piece onto brown paper (cut-up grocery bags are good for this). Measure six inches from bottom hem of jumper skirt all along skirt bottom. Draw line with bright magic marker and cut along line, dividing skirt into two separate pieces. Add ¼" seam allowance to bottom of skirt top and ¼" seam allowance to top of skirt bottom.

　2. Cut bib, bib linings, skirt front top, and skirt back top from red Trigger. Cut two skirt bottoms (front and back) and shoulder straps from royal blue Trigger.

　3. To appliqué bib, back white piqué and yellow Trigger with lightweight

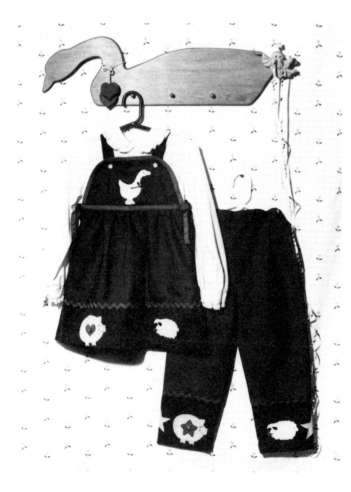

Fig. 4–3 Animal Crackers jumper and pants.

70

iron-on interfacing. Cut out goose body from white piqué and goose beak and feet from yellow Trigger. Position and pin goose body to center of bib front with beak and feet tucked in, per pattern. Mark wing, eye, and feet stitch details with water-soluble marking pen. Using medium-width zigzag satin stitch, appliqué body, beak, and feet, using bright yellow thread. Zigzag satin stitch wing and feet details. Embroider eye with two strands of light blue embroidery floss in satin stitch. Tie bow, using ⅛"-wide royal blue satin ribbon, and tack at bottom of goose's neck. Press.

4. Pin appliquéd bib to front bib lining with wrong sides together, and stitch around sides and bib top ⅛" from edge. Encase sides and bib top with extra-wide kelly green bias tape binding.

5. Pin bib back and bib back lining with wrong sides together and stitch around sides and bib top ⅛" from edge. Sew royal blue Trigger shoulder straps according to purchased pattern instructions. Position straps and baste to right side of bib back. Encase sides and bib top with extra-wide kelly green bias tape binding.

6. To appliqué blue skirt bottom, first back white piqué, black mini-dot fabric, red mini-dot fabric, pink heart print, and green dot fabric scraps with lightweight iron-on interfacing. Cut out appliqué pieces as follows:

2 hearts: red mini-dot fabric
2 pigs: pink heart fabric
2 small hearts: green dot fabric
2 lamb bodies: white piqué
2 lamb heads, 2 lamb ears, 2 pair front legs, and 2 pair back legs: black mini-dot fabric

Please note that some of these pieces should be cut in reverse, as indicated on the pattern piece.

7. Fold royal blue bottom skirt pieces vertically to find center front and center back. At center front fold, position, pin, and appliqué red mini-dot heart, using medium-width zigzag satin stitch.

8. Position, pin, and appliqué pig on middle of left front bottom with medium-width zigzag satin stitch. Pin green dot heart to center of pig body and appliqué with narrow width zigzag satin stitch. Using water-soluble marking pen, draw eye, nose, mouth, and tail. Using two strands of embroidery floss, embroider features: eye, light blue, back stitch; nose, hot pink, lazy daisy stitch; mouth, hot pink, working smile in, back stitch and heart in satin stitch; tail, hot pink, back stitch. Sew red heart button to center of green dot heart.

9. Position and pin lamb body on middle of right front bottom with face, front legs, and back legs tucked under white piqué body. Using medium-width zigzag satin stitch, appliqué around lamb body. With narrow zigzag satin stitch, appliqué face, front legs, and back legs. Position and appliqué ear. With two

strands of light blue embroidery floss, embroider eye using satin stitch. Press front bottom piece.

10. Appliqué back bottom piece, following instructions in Steps 7, 8, and 9 with pig on left, red mini-dot heart in center, and lamb on right. Press.

11. Pin bottom of skirt front top to top of skirt front bottom piece, with right sides together. Stitch seam, using ¼″ seam allowance, and press seam open. Repeat for back skirt section. Pin and stitch skirt side seams with right sides together, using ⅝″ seam allowance. Press seams open. Starting at right side seam connecting skirt top and skirt bottom, stitch kelly green jumbo rickrack along seam, tucking ends under and overlapping side seam. Press.

12. Gather skirt top to fit bib, matching fronts and backs at side seams. Adjust gathers and baste. Stitch skirt to bib, using ⅝″ seam allowance.

13. Cut two 45″ lengths of kelly green extra-wide bias tape. Fold pieces in middle and pin mark. Center pin mark of one length of bias tape to center of bib front along seam connecting bib to skirt. Baste bias tape to bib with ties extending on each side of bib. Stitch bias tape, using $^1/_{16}$″ seam allowance, along bias tape edge on both edges of tape. Tuck in tie ends for finished look and knot at ends. Repeat for back bib and tie bows at jumper sides.

14. Stitch yellow sun buttons to straps, at position indicated on your pattern. Mark buttonholes on bib front, according to pattern instructions, and make hand or machine buttonholes.

15. Sew tiny ¼″ brass bells under lamb heads. Tie two tiny bows, using ⅛″-wide red satin ribbon, and tack above bells.

16. Hem jumper according to pattern instructions. Press.

Variations

• Make jumper in spring pastel colors, substituting bunny for pig appliqué.
• Appliqué animals to purchased bib jumper or bib overalls; trim legs or skirt with ribbons and rickrack along with overall or jumper straps.
• If your favorite child prefers skirts, use skirt pattern for jumper used in Step 1 and extend top of skirt 2″ for both front and back skirt pieces. Make jumper skirt according to Steps 6, 7, 8, 9, 10, and 11. Fold under skirt top ¼″ and fold again 1½″. Pin and stitch casing; thread, and overlap elastic ends ½″, and stitch ends securely. Hand stitch casing closed.

ANIMAL CRACKERS PANTS

Choose a simple purchased pants pattern with waistband front and elastic back waist for the pants shown in Fig. 4-3.

■ Cost of materials: $9.00
■ Retail cost: $28.00

Materials

1 purchased pants pattern with waistband front and elastic back waist
⅝ yard red Trigger
¼ yard royal blue Trigger
   (for child's size 6; check pattern instructions for amounts needed)
1 yard kelly green jumbo rickrack
¼ yard ½"-wide elastic
Lightweight iron-on interfacing
Scraps of:
   kelly green Trigger
   white piqué
   black mini-dot fabric
   pink heart print fabric
   green dot fabric
   bright yellow Trigger
   ⅛"-wide red satin ribbon
1 red ¾" star button
2 tiny ¼" brass bells
2 gold ½" star buttons
Embroidery floss in light blue, royal blue, and hot pink
Water-soluble marking pen
Matching threads

Directions

1. Trace pant leg pattern (front and back) onto brown paper (cut-up grocery bags are good for this). Measure 7½" from bottom hem of pant leg all along bottom. Draw line with bright magic marker, and cut along line dividing leg into two separate pieces. Repeat for both legs, front and back. Tape pant bottom pieces together, overlapping outer leg side seams to make one long piece. Add ¼" seam allowance to top of bottom pants leg pieces and ¼" seam allowance to top pieces' bottom edges.

2. Cut waistband from kelly green Trigger, pants front and back tops from red Trigger, and pant bottom pieces (cut 2, 1 for each leg) from royal blue Trigger.

3. To appliqué royal blue bottom piece, back yellow Trigger, white piqué, black mini-dot fabric, pink heart print fabric, and green dot fabric scraps with lightweight iron-on interfacing. Cut out appliqué pieces as follows:

2 stars: yellow Trigger
1 goose body: white piqué

1 goose beak, and 1 pair goose feet: yellow Trigger
2 lamb bodies: white piqué
2 lamb heads, 2 lamb ears, 2 pair front legs, and 2 pair back legs: black mini-dot fabric
1 pig: pink heart print fabric
1 small star: green dot fabric

Please note that some of these pieces should be cut in reverse, as indicated on the patterns.

4. Fold right pant bottom in half vertically to center and to mark outer side seam. At fold, position, pin, and appliqué yellow star to center with medium-width zigzag satin stitch. Position and pin lamb body to middle of left pant bottom with lamb facing left; face, front legs, and back legs should be tucked under white piqué body. Using medium-width zigzag satin stitch, appliqué around lamb body. With narrow zigzag satin stitch, appliqué face, front legs, and back legs. Position and appliqué ear. With two strands royal blue embroidery floss, embroider eye using satin stitch.

5. Position and pin goose body to middle of right of star appliqué on pant bottom piece, with goose facing to right. Tuck in goose beak and feet per pattern. Mark eye, wing, and feet details to be stitched, using water-soluble marking pen. Using medium-width zigzag satin stitch, appliqué body, beak, and feet, using bright yellow thread. Zigzag satin stitch wing and feet details. Embroider eye with two strands royal blue embroidery floss in satin stitch. Tie bow, using ⅛"-wide red satin ribbon, and tack at bottom of goose's neck. Press.

6. Fold left pant bottom piece in half vertically to center and to mark outer side seam. At fold, position, pin, and appliqué yellow star to center with medium-width zigzag satin stitch. Position and pin lamb body to middle of left leg, with lamb facing right; face, front legs, and back legs should be tucked under white piqué body. Using medium-width zigzag satin stitch, appliqué around lamb body. With narrow zigzag satin stitch, appliqué face, front legs, and back legs. Position and appliqué ear. With two strands royal blue embroidery floss, embroider eye using satin stitch.

7. Position and pin pig to middle of right star appliqué on bottom pant leg, with pig facing right. Appliqué pig with medium-width zigzag satin stitch. Using water-soluble marking pen, draw in eye, nose, mouth, and tail. Using two strands embroidery floss, embroider features: eyes, light blue, back stitch; nose, hot pink, lazy daisy stitch; mouth, hot pink, back stitch, and heart in satin stitch. Sew red star button to center of green dot star. Press.

8. Follow purchased pattern instructions to assemble pants, but *do not sew* crotch seam. Press outer leg seams open. Pin top pant leg to bottom pant leg with right sides together and stitch seam with ¼" seam allowance. Press seam open.

9. Stitch kelly green jumbo rickrack along pant top and bottom, connecting seam.

10. Repeat for other pant leg. Stitch crotch seam, using ⅝″ seam allowance per purchased pattern instructions.

11. Sew tiny ¼″ brass bell under lamb head. Tie tiny bow, using ⅛″-wide red satin ribbon, and tack above bell. Repeat for other lamb. Sew gold star buttons on outer ends of waistband.

12. Hem according to purchased pattern instructions. Press.

ANIMAL CRACKERS SWEATER

The sweater is shown on the cover and in the color section.

- Cost of materials: $12.00
- Retail cost: $30.00

Materials

Purchased yellow crewneck sweater, acrylic or washable wool
Lightweight iron-on interfacing
Scraps of:
   white piqué
   brown mini-dot fabric
   tan and white mini-floral print
   pink heart print fabric
   ⅛″-wide red satin ribbon
1 yellow ⅝″ sun button
1 small cow bell
Embroidery floss in brown, light pink, and red
Water-soluble marking pen
Matching threads

Directions

1. Cut piece of lightweight iron-on interfacing 10″ × 9″ and fuse to center of *wrong* side of sweater front. This procedure stabilizes the sweater knit so it does not stretch while appliquéing. Be sure to use a ballpoint sewing machine needle in your machine for best results.

2. To appliqué sweater, back white piqué, brown mini-dot fabric, tan and white mini-floral print, and pink heart print fabric scraps with lightweight iron-on interfacing. Cut out appliqué pieces as follows:

1 cloud: white piqué
1 cow body: brown mini-dot fabric
1 cow head: tan and white mini-floral print
1 cow mouth and 1 cow hind spot: white piqué
1 udder: pink heart print

3. Position, pin, and appliqué white piqué cloud to upper righthand side of

sweater front, using medium-width zigzag satin stitch. Sew yellow sun button to righthand side of cloud, so it looks like sun is peeking out.

4. Position and pin cow body to center of sweater front, tucking in udder on right lower side of cow, per pattern. Appliqué cow body and udder, using medium-width zigzag satin stitch. Position, pin, and appliqué cow hind spot per pattern, using medium-width zigzag satin stitch. Position and pin cow head and mouth at a jaunty angle; appliqué using narrow zigzag satin stitch. Using water-soluble marking pen, draw in eyes, nose, mouth, and tail. Using two strands of embroidery floss, embroider features: eyes, brown, satin stitch; nose, hot pink, satin stitch; mouth, red, working smile in back stitch and hearts in satin stitch; tail, brown, back stitch.

5. Sew cow bell just under cow's head. Tie tiny bow, using ⅛"-wide red satin ribbon, and tack above bell.

6. Steam press sweater, using pressing cloth.

Six Super Snazzy Sweaters

All the sweaters shown in this section are acrylic crewnecks and cardigans manufactured by Bluebird Knitwear. These sweaters wash beautifully and wear extremely well; I recommend them without reservation. Washable wool sweaters also work well.

The designs and color selections I've used are just the tip of the iceberg: sweaters can be personalized, ribbon-trimmed, appliquéd with scenes, animals, flowers, sports motifs, and so on.

Prewash all sweaters according to manufacturer's instructions to be sure sweater dyes are colorfast. Lightly steam press with press cloth if necessary. When laundering appliquéd and trimmed sweaters, turn them wrong-side-out before tossing in the washer: this helps to reduce pilling or snagging other clothing in washer.

RUFFLES & RIBBONS & BUTTONS & BOWS SWEATER

This delightful back-to-school sweater is shown in Fig. 4-4. Collect favorite buttons and you'll be surprised how quickly you'll have enough for this sweater.

NOTE: It is not recommended for children under 3 years old.

- Cost of materials: $25.00
- Retail cost: $49.50

Materials
   1 purchased navy blue acrylic cardigan sweater
   2 yards ½"-wide navy blue and red "apple" woven ribbon
   2 yards 1"-wide white eyelet ruffled lace trim
   32 multicolored novelty buttons:

Fig. 4–4 Ruffles & Ribbons & Buttons & Bows Sweater. Photo by Marnie Leonard.

7 yellow
8 red
3 hot pink
2 purple
5 green
3 white
4 brown
Matching threads

Directions

1. Stitch apple ribbon over edge of eyelet binding to make ribbon-trimmed eyelet lace.

2. Starting just above ribbing at bottom of sweater, baste ribbon-trimmed eyelet lace around sweater bottom. Stitch top and bottom edges of ribbon to sweater. *Do not stitch* through eyelet (see Diag. 4-6).

3. Hand baste ribbon-trimmed eyelet lace around armholes, just at set-in sleeve seam. Stitch top and bottom edges of ribbon to sweater. *Do not stitch* through eyelet.

4. Remove buttons originally on sweater and set aside. Replace the buttons in the following color order: red, yellow, green, brown, red, and green. If you are making a large size, continue with white and yellow buttons.

5. Scatter remaining buttons on the front left and right sides of the sweater so that the colors are spread out and appealing to the eye. If you have a difficult time doing this, refer to color photograph of sweaters. Pin buttons in place and sew each on *securely;* this sweater will quickly become a favorite and will be laundered repeatedly!

This sweater has always been a favorite in our home. As the sweater is outgrown, I snip off the buttons, add a few new favorites, and make another one for the coming school year. Watch for special novelty buttons in stationery stores, gift shops, and dime stores. The assortment of novelty button trims is wide: our favorites include sunglasses, Coke bottles, and telephones.

DAISIES ARE FOREVER SWEATER

This charming sweater is shown in Fig. 4-5.

- Cost of materials: $13.50
- Retail cost: $27.50

Materials

1 purchased red acrylic crewneck sweater
1/8 yard red plaid fabric
1/8 yard white with red heart flower print fabric
1/8 yard navy blue mini-floral print fabric
1/4 yard stiff fusible interfacing
1/4 yard Stitch Witchery
Scraps of:
    red mini-dot fabric
    yellow Trigger
    kelly green Trigger
Matching threads

Fig. 4–5 Daisy sweater.
Photo by Marnie Leonard.

Directions

1. To make daisies, fuse fabrics in the following manner: fuse 4″ x 8″ pieces of stiff iron-on interfacing to *wrong* side of red plaid, white with heart flower print, and navy blue mini-floral print fabrics. Use a sheet of tissue paper between fused fabrics and iron to avoid sticky build-up on your iron. Fuse 4″-square pieces of stiff iron-on interfacing to wrong side of red mini-dot, yellow Trigger, and green Trigger.

2. Make a sandwich of the fused fabrics. Using red plaid as an example: red plaid right-side-down, Stitch Witchery in middle, and red plaid right-side-up. Place a sheet of tissue paper over "sandwich." Set iron for cotton and hold iron over sandwich stack until bond is secure. Turn over and repeat.

3. Fuse sandwiches of white with red heart flower print, navy blue mini-floral print fabric, and kelly green Trigger as in Step 2. When all fabrics are fused (and made reversible), you are all set to make the daisies.

4. Trace daisy pattern and glue to piece of stiff paper. Cut out daisy pattern and trace around daisies, using sharp #2 pencil. Make 2 red plaid daisies, 2 navy blue print daisies, and 1 white with red heart flower print daisy for the sweater. (I always make 4 to 6 additional daisies to have on hand; see suggestions at end of this project.)

5. Carefully cut out all daisies along pencil lines. Cut out red mini-dot and

yellow Trigger daisy centers to match the number of daisies you are making. Note that only the red plaid daisies have yellow Trigger centers. Cut out leaves from green Trigger to match daisies.

6. Thread sewing machine with matching top and bobbin threads to match each color of daisy. Starting with red plaid daisy, using wide zigzag satin stitch, zigzag around outside edges of each daisy. Zigzag satin stitch around leaves, using medium-width stitch. Clip all threads from daisies and leaves.

7. Position daisies as shown in Fig. 4-5, with three daisies around neckline: two on the left and one on the right, just below neckline ribbing. From left to right, use white with red heart flower print daisy, red plaid daisy, and navy blue mini-floral print daisy. Place leaf under each daisy so that end of leaf is under center of daisy. Position center of daisy in center of flower and pin through daisy center, daisy, and leaf. Using wide zigzag satin stitch, appliqué daisy center so it secures daisy, leaf, and center to sweater. Clip threads. Complete all three neckline daisies in this manner.

8. Position navy blue mini-floral print daisy at left wrist, just above ribbing and opposite underarm seam. Appliqué as described in Step. 7.

9. Position red plaid daisy on bottom right of sweater, just above ribbing. Stitch as described in Step 7. Clip all threads.

Daisy Accessories

For extra daisies, place leaf under each daisy so that end of leaf is under center of daisy. Position center of daisy in center of flower and pin through daisy center, daisy, and leaf. Appliqué center to daisy. Turn daisy over and trim any excess leaf away from center to ease bulk. Sew machine buttonhole through center of daisy, tie off threads, and slit.

These extra daisies may be buttoned onto a Bermuda bag for a very special touch. Or, if you have a pigtailed little darling, use small ball ponytail holders; carefully button daisies over ponytail balls, and your child will have daisies in her hair. You can also glue daisy centers to ribbon-trimmed headbands.

Why not spiff up those sneakers or oxfords by threading the shoelaces through the center of the daisy buttonhole and tying laces into a bow? The uses for the delightful daisies are unlimited.

TIPTOE THROUGH THE TULIPS SWEATER

A floral theme enhances the sweater shown in Fig. 4-6.

- Cost of materials: $12.00
- Retail cost: $30.00

Materials
  1 navy blue acrylic crewneck sweater
  Scraps of:
    red mini-dot fabric

Fig. 4-6 Tiptoe through the Tulips Sweater. Photo by Marnie Leonard.

white piqué
kelly green Trigger
Stitch Witchery
Lightweight iron-on interfacing
2 white ½" heart buttons
Matching threads

Directions

1. Cut piece of lightweight iron-on interfacing 10" x 6" and fuse to wrong side of sweater front at upper center. This procedure stabilizes the sweater knit, to prevent stretching while appliquéing. Be sure to use a ballpoint sewing machine needle in your machine for best results.

2. Back white piqué, red mini-dot fabric, and green Trigger fabric scraps with lightweight iron-on interfacing. Cut out appliqué pieces as follows:

1 large heart: white piqué
1 small heart and 2 tulips: red mini-dot fabric
2 stems, 2 small leaves, and 2 large leaves: green Trigger

Please note that some pieces should be cut in reverse, as indicated on patterns.

3. Pin mark the center front of sweater. Position and pin large white piqué heart under pin mark to upper center of sweater. Appliqué white piqué heart, us-

81

ing medium-width zigzag satin stitch. Position and appliqué small red mini-dot heart to center of white piqué heart, using narrow zigzag satin stitch.

4. Position stems, leaves, and tulips on each side of hearts. Spread out for larger sizes, make more compact for smaller sizes. Snip tiny pieces of Stitch Witchery and tuck under tulip, stem, and leaves. Place pressing cloth over appliqué; steam iron to set. Using the Stitch Witchery will help hold the skinny stem and little pieces so you won't have trouble with them moving while appliquéing.

5. Appliqué tulip, stem, and leaves, using medium-width zigzag satin stitch. Sew white heart button over tulip on each side.

APPLE OF MY EYE SWEATER

Your little one will be teacher's favorite, indeed, wearing the sweater shown in Fig. 4-7.

- Cost of materials: $11.00
- Retail cost: $20.00

Materials
    1 yellow acrylic crewneck sweater
    Lightweight iron-on interfacing

Fig. 4–7 Apple of My Eye Sweater. Photo by Marnie Leonard.

82

Scraps of:
  red mini-dot fabric
  brown mini-dot fabric
  green Trigger
1 "squiggly" worm button
Matching threads

Directions

1. Cut piece of lightweight iron-on interfacing slightly larger than appliqué size and fuse to *wrong* side at upper right side of sweater front. This procedure stabilizes the sweater knit so it does not stretch while appliquéing. Be sure to use a ballpoint sewing machine needle for best results.

2. To appliqué sweater, back red mini-dot fabric, brown mini-dot fabric and green Trigger fabric scraps with lightweight iron-on interfacing. Cut out appliqué pieces as follows:

1 apple: red mini-dot fabric
1 stem: brown mini-dot fabric
1 leaf: green Trigger

3. Position and pin apple appliqué and tuck in brown mini-dot stem per pattern. Appliqué apple, using medium-width zigzag satin stitch. With narrow zigzag satin stitch, appliqué stem. Position, pin, and appliqué leaf at an angle to the right of the stem, using medium-width zigzag satin stitch. Topstitch vein down middle of leaf.

4. Sew "squiggly" worm button on right upper side of apple.

ANCHORS AWEIGH SWEATER

Other nautical buttons can be substituted if you cannot find the same ones I used on the sweater in Fig. 4-8.

- Cost of materials: $12.00
- Retail cost: $20.00

Materials

1 navy blue acrylic crewneck sweater
2 red anchor buttons
3 gold ⅜" star buttons
1 red ship's wheel button
Scraps of:
  white piqué
  ⅛"-wide red satin ribbon
Lightweight iron-on interfacing
Matching threads

Fig. 4–8 Anchors Aweigh Sweater. Photo by Marnie Leonard.

Directions

1. Cut piece of lightweight iron-on interfacing slightly larger than anchor appliqué; fuse to *wrong* side at upper right side of sweater front. This procedure stabilizes the sweater knit while appliquéing. Be sure to use a ballpoint sewing machine needle for best results.

2. Back white piqué fabric with lightweight iron-on interfacing and cut out anchor appliqué. Position and pin anchor, tucking in 3″ piece of ⅛″ red satin ribbon at left top side of anchor, per pattern. Appliqué anchor, using medium-width

84

zigzag satin stitch; catch bottom of ribbon on left bottom side of anchor. Stitch this appliqué slowly because of all the turns, points, and small areas.

3. Tack ⅛″ red satin ribbon to right side of anchor, as in photograph, and sew gold star button at tacked point.

4. Trim front neckline just under ribbing with nautical buttons; from left to right: red anchor, gold star, red ship's wheel in center, gold star, and red anchor. Space buttons evenly and sew in place.

PUPPY LOVE SWEATER

Puppy isn't the only one who'll adore this sweater (Fig 4-9).

- Cost of materials: $11.00
- Retail cost: $22.50

Materials
1 burgundy acrylic crewneck sweater
Lightweight iron-on interfacing
Scraps of:
    brown and burgundy print fabric
    tan with blue mini-dot fabric

Fig. 4–9 Puppy Love Sweater. Photo by Marnie Leonard.

burgundy mini-dot fabric
    black acrylic felt
Pink Venus pencil
Black embroidery thread
Matching threads

Directions

1. Cut piece of lightweight iron-on interfacing slightly larger than puppy appliqué, and fuse to *wrong* side at upper right side of sweater front. This procedure stabilizes the sweater knit, to keep it from stretching while appliquéing. Be sure to use a ballpoint sewing machine needle for best results.

2. Cut two right and two left puppy ears from brown and burgundy print fabric, per pattern pieces. With right sides together, stitch around puppy ears with 1/8" seam allowance, leaving open, per pattern. Turn puppy ears right-side-out and press.

3. Back brown and burgundy print fabric, tan with blue mini-dot fabric, and burgundy mini-dot fabric with lightweight iron-on interfacing. Cut out appliqué pieces as follows:

1 puppy face: tan with blue mini-dot
1 puppy face spot: brown and burgundy print
1 puppy nose and 1 puppy tongue: burgundy mini-dot
2 eyes: black acrylic felt

4. Position and pin puppy face, tucking in ears on sides so that ears can flop and tuck in tongue under center bottom of puppy face. Using medium-width zig-zag satin stitch, appliqué face. Position, pin, and appliqué puppy face spot on left upper side of puppy face with medium-width zigzag satin stitch. Position, pin, and appliqué nose and tongue, using narrow zigzag satin stitch. Tack eyes in place as shown on pattern piece. Embroider eyelashes and eyebrows, using two strands of black embroidery floss in straight stitch.

5. Embroider puppy smile in burgundy thread, using double thread with french knots on ends. Lightly shade puppy cheeks with pink Venus pencil.

86

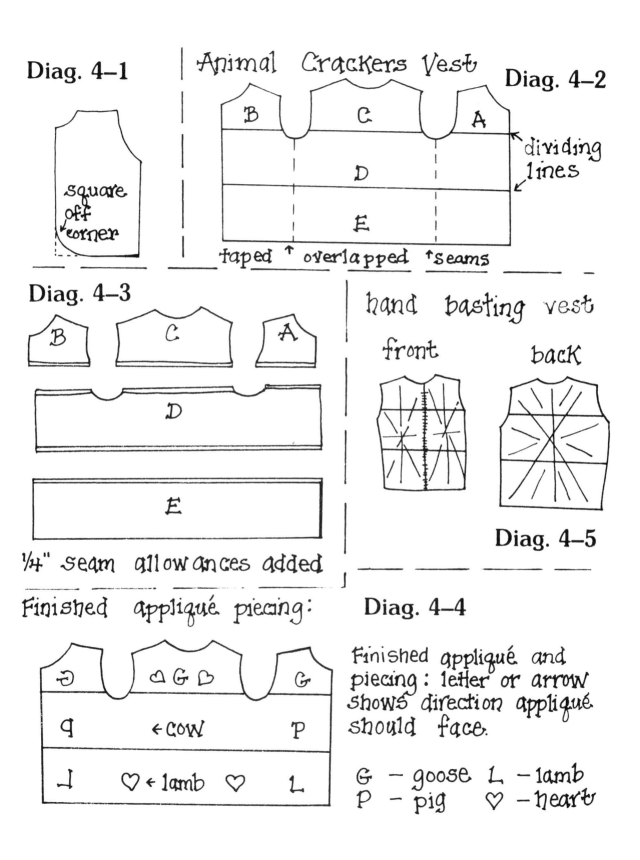

Diag. 4-1

square off corner

Animal Crackers Vest

Diag. 4-2

B   C   A

← dividing lines

D

E

taped ↑ overlapped ↑ seams

Diag. 4-3

B   C   A

D

E

¼" seam allowances added

hand basting vest

front   back

Diag. 4-5

Finished appliqué piecing:

G   ◁ G ▷   G

q   ← cow   P

⌐   ♡ ← lamb ♡   L

Diag. 4-4

Finished appliqué and piecing: letter or arrow shows direction appliqué should face.

G — goose   L — lamb
P — pig   ♡ — heart

Animal Crackers Appliqué Patterns

large heart

beak

feet

Cut 1 each per goose bright yellow Trigger

goose appliqué placement pattern

zigzag stitch detail

goose

white piqué

attach bow here.

GOOSE PATTERN

For Vest

Cut 3 goose bodies, white piqué: 1 facing left, 2 facing right

Cut 3 goose beaks, bright yellow Trigger: 1 facing left, 2 facing right

Cut 3 pair goose feet, bright yellow Trigger: 1 facing left, 2 facing right

For Jumper

Cut 1 goose body, white piqué, facing right

Cut 1 goose beak, bright yellow Trigger, facing right

Cut 1 pair goose feet, bright yellow Trigger, facing right

For Pants

Cut 1 goose body, white piqué, facing right

Cut 1 goose beak, bright yellow Trigger, facing right

Cut 1 pair goose feet, bright yellow Trigger, facing right

Animal Crackers Appliqué Patterns

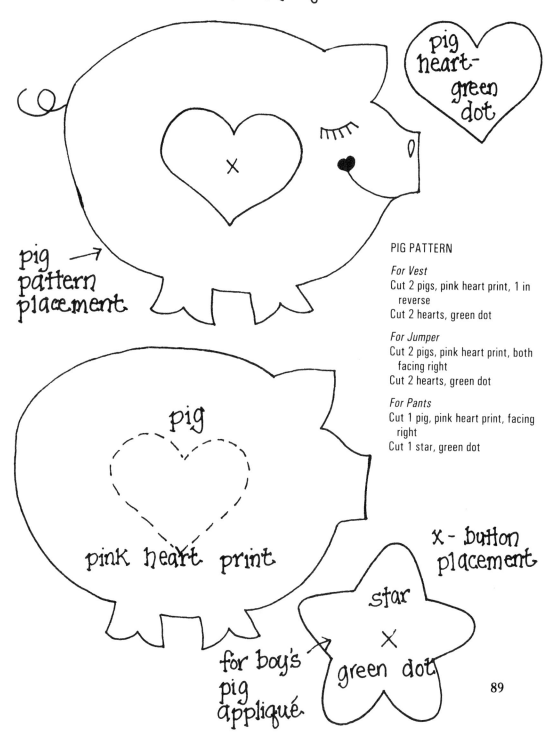

pig heart–
green dot

pig pattern placement.

PIG PATTERN

For Vest
Cut 2 pigs, pink heart print, 1 in reverse
Cut 2 hearts, green dot

For Jumper
Cut 2 pigs, pink heart print, both facing right
Cut 2 hearts, green dot

For Pants
Cut 1 pig, pink heart print, facing right
Cut 1 star, green dot

pig

pink heart print

X – button placement

star
X
green dot

for boy's pig appliqué.

89

Animal Crackers Appliqué Patterns

star
cut 2
yellow
Trigger
for pants

Note:
If making
vest for
boy- cut
2 stars
yellow mini-dot for piece.
C and
2 stars red
mini-dot
for piece
E.

cloud
white piqué X
for sweater

sun button placement

tan
mini-floral

cow
head

hind spot-
white
piqué

cow mouth-white piqué

X = Cow bell
and bow
placement

cow body
brown mini-dot.

udder

pink heart
print

90

Cow Appliqué Placement Pattern

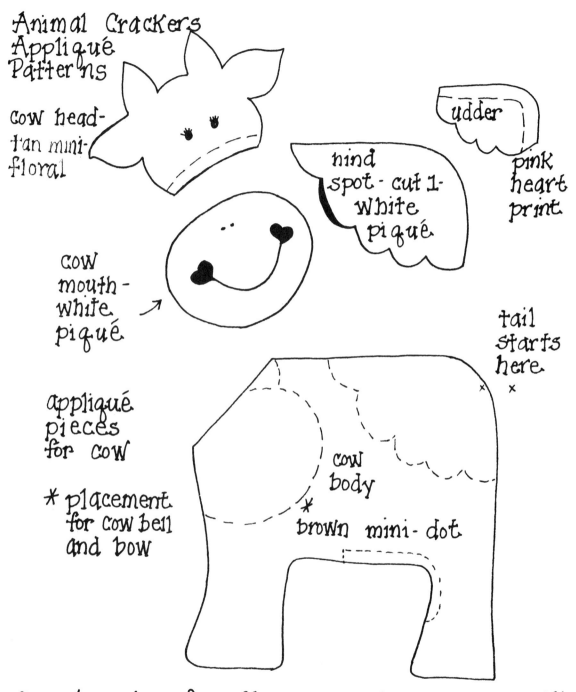

Animal Crackers
Appliqué
Patterns

cow head-
tan mini-
floral

udder

pink
heart
print

hind
spot - cut 1-
white
piqué

cow
mouth -
white
piqué

tail
starts
here

appliqué
pieces
for cow

cow
body

* placement
for cow bell
and bow

* brown mini - dot

Cut 1 each of patterns as shown above with
cow facing left:
91
    cut 1 complete cow for vest
    cut 1 complete cow for sweater

Animal Crackers Appliqué Patterns

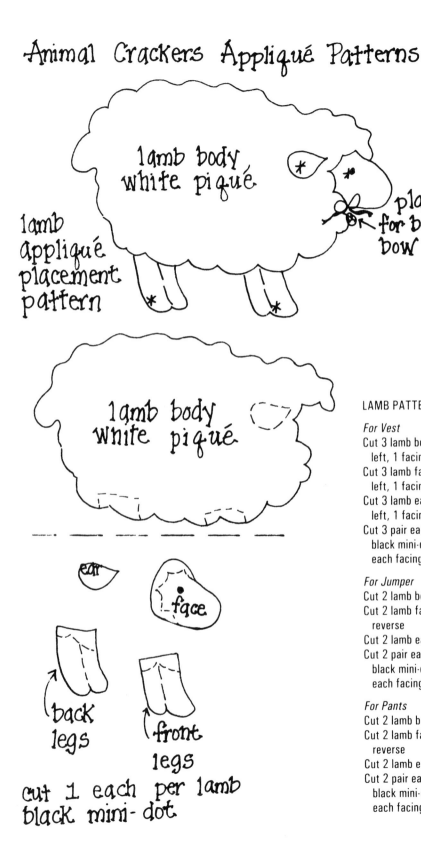

lamb body
white piqué

lamb
appliqué
placement
pattern

placement
for bell and
bow

lamb body
white piqué

ear

face

back
legs

front
legs

cut 1 each per lamb
black mini-dot.

LAMB PATTERN

For Vest

Cut 3 lamb bodies, white piqué: 2 facing
    left, 1 facing right
Cut 3 lamb faces, black mini-dot: 2 facing
    left, 1 facing right
Cut 3 lamb ears, black mini-dot: 2 facing
    left, 1 facing right
Cut 3 pair each front and back lamb legs,
    black mini-dot: 2 of each facing left, 1 of
    each facing right

For Jumper

Cut 2 lamb bodies, white piqué: 1 in reverse
Cut 2 lamb faces, black mini-dot: 1 in
    reverse
Cut 2 lamb ears, black mini-dot: 1 in reverse
Cut 2 pair each front and back lamb legs,
    black mini-dot: 1 of each facing left, 1 of
    each facing right

For Pants

Cut 2 lamb bodies, white piqué: 1 in reverse
Cut 2 lamb faces, black mini-dot: 1 in
    reverse
Cut 2 lamb ears, black mini-dot: 1 in reverse
Cut 2 pair each lamb front and back legs,
    black mini-dot: 1 of each facing left, 1 of
    each facing right

Diag. 4-6 Drawing of Ruffles & Ribbons & Buttons & Bows Sweater

small daisy

small daisy leaf

small daisy center

large daisy center

large daisy

large daisy leaf

Appliqués for Daisies Are Forever Sweater

Note: Small daisy appliqués are for sizes Infant to Child Size 4.

Large daisy appliqués are for sizes Child Size 5 and up.

93

Tiptoe Through The Tulips Appliqué Patterns

large heart
cut 1
white piqué

*left side leaf
cut 2
1 in reverse

*stem - cut 2 - 1 in reverse

tulip
cut 2
red
mini-dot

*right side leaf
cut 2
1 in reverse

Size small for
Infants through
Child Size 6

small heart
cut 1
red &
mini-dot

size large for
Child Size 7
through Adult

* cut from
Kelly green
Trigger

tulip
cut 2
red
mini-dot

*right side leaf
cut 2
1 in reverse

large heart
white piqué
cut 1

*left side leaf
*1 in reverse
cut 2

stem - cut 2 - 1 in reverse - green Trigger

small heart
cut 1
red
mini-dot

94

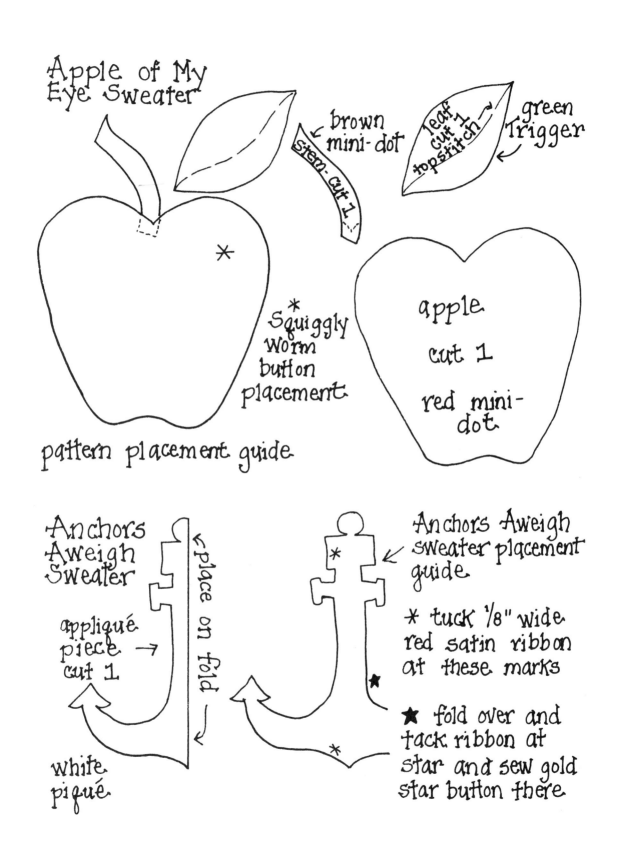

Apple of My Eye Sweater

brown mini-dot

stem cut 1

leaf cut 1 topstitch

green Trigger

*
Squiggly worm button placement

apple cut 1 red mini-dot

pattern placement guide

Anchors Aweigh Sweater

appliqué piece cut 1

place on fold

white piqué

Anchors Aweigh sweater placement guide

* tuck 1/8" wide red satin ribbon at these marks

★ fold over and tack ribbon at star and sew gold star button there

Puppy Love Sweater

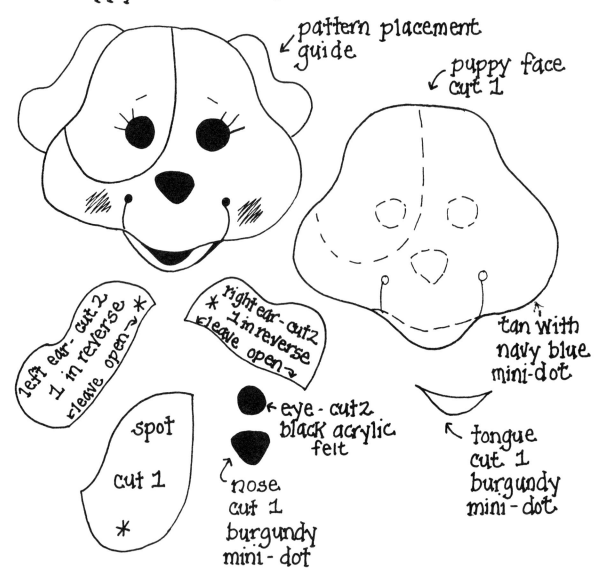

pattern placement guide

puppy face cut 1

left ear - cut 2 1 in reverse ~leave open~ *

* right ear - cut 2 1 in reverse ~leave open~

tan with navy blue mini-dot

eye - cut 2 black acrylic felt

spot

cut 1

*

nose cut 1 burgundy mini-dot

tongue cut 1 burgundy mini-dot

Note: ears have ⅛" seam allowance **included**.

* brown and burgundy print fabric

CHAPTER 5

Winter Wonderland:
Visions of Sugarplums

As Jack Frost snips his first snowflake of the season, I hear sleigh bells in the distance, smell the faint aroma of holiday treats fresh from the oven, and envision eight tiny reindeer pulling a sleigh packed to overflowing — gliding past the moon on a bright, clear Christmas Eve. Teddy bear stockings are hung by the chimney with care, knowing that loving delights will soon be there.

The tiny finery, treasured totes, and stocking stuffers in this chapter cover a wide range of holiday gift-giving needs. Reach for pencil and paper and start your Christmas list here!

SNIP THE SNOWMAN APPLIQUÉD JUMPER

Choose a simple A-line jumper pattern. The jumper shown in Fig. 5-1 has a square neckline and armholes, and is completely lined. Depending upon your climate, you can make the jumper in fabrics ranging from Trigger to corduroy to washable wool. To make the jumper for dressy occasions, use no-wale corduroy or velveteen.

- Cost of materials: $10.00
- Retail cost: $35.00

Materials
Purchased A-line jumper pattern
½ yard navy blue Trigger
½ yard red mini-dot fabric
    (fabrics based on toddler's size 3; check pattern instructions for amount needed.)
Lightweight iron-on interfacing
2 white ½" heart buttons
1 white ½" pompom
Scraps of:
    white piqué
    red mini-dot
    red plaid fabric

Fig. 5–1 Snip the Snowman jumper and purse.

    orange Trigger
    green Trigger
  Embroidery floss in black and red
  Water-soluble marking pen
  Matching threads

Directions

    1. Per purchased pattern instructions, cut jumper front and back from navy blue Trigger and red mini-dot fabric.

98

2. Back white piqué, red mini-dot, red plaid, kelly green Trigger, and orange Trigger fabric scraps with lightweight iron-on interfacing. Cut out appliqué pieces as follows:

1 snowman body: white piqué
1 snowman hat and heart cheek: red mini-dot
snowman earmuffs and 3 buttons: green Trigger
carrot nose: orange Trigger
snowman scarf: red plaid

3. With water-soluble marking pen, draw in snowman eyes, smile, and topstitching lines for arms and legs.

4. Position and pin snowman body to middle of jumper front and appliqué in place, using medium-width zigzag satin stitch. Topstitch arm and leg markings, using zigzag satin stitch . Position, pin, and stitch snowman appliqués in the following order, using medium-width zigzag satin stitch: hat, left earmuff, right earmuff, carrot nose, scarf, and three green buttons down front of body.

5. With two strands of black embroidery floss, embroider eyes, using satin stitch; embroider smile with red floss in stem stitch. Appliqué heart cheek to end of smile, using narrow-width zigzag satin stitch. Press. Tack white pompom to end of cap.

6. Following purchased pattern instructions, line and assemble jumper. Use ½" white heart buttons at shoulders. Press.

Variations

- This appliqué is well suited to boys clothing, too. Appliqué snowman on shortalls, overalls, sweatsuits, or sleepwear. When appliquéing to sweatshirt, add a few snowflake sequins or dab on a few drops of white acrylic paint to make snow falling in sky and around Snip.
- Use the small version of this appliqué, shown on pattern placement page, to embellish scarf ends, small tote bags, or hand towels. It is also ideal for bibs on overalls or jumpers.

SNIP THE SNOWMAN PURSE

The purse is shown in Fig. 5-1, along with the jumper.

- Cost of materials: $5.00
- Retail cost: $12.50

Materials
¼ yard white sweatshirt fleece knit
¼ yard white with red mini-dot fabric
1 yard ½"-wide green velvet ribbon
1 white ½" pompom
2 green ½" pompoms

3 green ¼" pompoms
1 red ⅛" round wooden bead
1 white ½" Velcro dot set
Lightweight iron-on interfacing
Scraps of:
   red mini-dot fabric
   green acrylic felt
   red plaid fabric
   orange Trigger
Embroidery floss in black and red
Water-soluble marking pen
Hot glue gun and glue sticks
Matching threads

Directions

1. Cut two white fleece snowmen (one in reverse) and two white with red dot fabric snowmen (one in reverse). Back the white fleece snowman facing left with lightweight iron-on interfacing. This procedure stabilizes the sweatshirt fleece knit. Be sure to use a ballpoint sewing machine needle for best results.

2. For appliquéing snowman purse front, back red mini-dot fabric, red plaid fabric, and orange Trigger fabric scraps with lightweight iron-on interfacing. Cut out appliqué pieces as follows:

1 snowman cap and 1 heart cheek: red mini-dot
1 scarf: red plaid fabric
1 carrot nose: orange Trigger

3. Per placement drawing, appliqué red mini-dot hat, red plaid scarf, and orange carrot nose, using medium-width zigzag satin stitch. Using water-soluble marking pen, draw in eyes and smile. Embroider eyes in satin stitch, using two strands black floss; embroider smile in stem stitch, using two strands red embroidery floss. Appliqué red mini-dot heart cheek to end of smile, using narrow zigzag satin stitch. Lightly press.

4. Pin appliquéd purse front to lining front, right sides together. Stitch around perimeter, using ⅛" seam allowance, leaving open per pattern piece. Clip curves and corners, turn, and hand stitch closed. Repeat for purse back.

5. Cut out four snowman feet (two in reverse) and pin, right sides together. Stitch, using ⅛" seam allowance, leaving open per pattern piece; turn right-side-out.

6. Pin snowman purse with right sides of linings facing and tuck in feet, per pattern piece. Be sure to match up the snowman halves as perfectly as possible. Cut ½"-wide green velvet ribbon into 26" piece and tuck ends in at upper arms to make shoulder strap for purse.

7. Starting at right side of scarf ends, topstitch around perimeter of snowman, using ⅛" seam allowance, to where scarf starts on the left side.

8. Tie bow, using remaining amount of green velvet ribbon, and tack 8" above righthand strap. Cut two holly leaves from green acrylic felt and hot glue to lower right edge of cap. Hot glue red wooden bead just under leaves as holly berry. Hot glue ½" green pompoms just under each side of cap for earmuffs and hot glue three green ¼" pompoms down body front as buttons.

9. Hand stitch Velcro dot fasteners to inside top of cap to hold purse closed. Fill with little goodies like candy canes, fancy pencils and erasers, and a roll of new pennies for a special treat.

JINGLES THE REINDEER SWEATER

This bright, perky reindeer was inspired by one of our favorite cookie cutters and came to life with snips of fabric and trim. The sweater (Fig. 5-2) makes a great accompaniment to the Personalized Pants.

- Cost of materials: $12.00
- Retail cost: $27.50

Materials

Purchased green acrylic crewneck sweater
Lightweight iron-on interfacing
5 gold ⅜" sleigh bell buttons
1 red ⅛" pompom

Fig. 5–2 Jingles the Reindeer Sweater. Photo by Marnie Leonard.

Scraps of:
> brown mini-dot fabric
> red mini-dot fabric
> red and white mini-stripe fabric
> ⅛"-wide red satin ribbon

Embroidery floss in black and red
Matching threads

Directions

1. Cut piece of lightweight iron-on interfacing 6" × 6" and fuse to *wrong* side of sweater at center front. This procedure stabilizes the sweater knit so it does not stretch while appliquéing. Be sure to use a ballpoint sewing machine needle for best results.

2. To appliqué sweater, back brown mini-dot, red mini-dot, and red and white mini-stripe fabric scraps with lightweight iron-on interfacing. Cut out appliqué pieces as follows:

1 reindeer body and 2 ears: brown mini-dot
2 antlers: red mini-dot
1 scarf: red and white mini-stripe

3. Position and pin reindeer body to center of sweater, tucking in antlers, per pattern placement. Appliqué around reindeer body, using medium-width zigzag satin stitch. Appliqué around antlers with medium to narrow zigzag satin stitch. Position, pin, and appliqué reindeer ears per pattern placement, using narrow zigzag satin stitch. Position, pin, and appliqué scarf, using medium to narrow-width zigzag satin stitch.

4. Using water-soluble marking pen, draw in eyes, eyebrows, and smile. Using two strands of floss, embroider features: eyes, black, satin stitch; eyebrows, black, straight stitch; mouth, red, back stitch. Tack ⅛" red pompom in place for nose. Sew sleight bell button at neck of reindeer.

5. Position four sleigh bell buttons around neck front, just below ribbing, and sew in place. Using ⅛" red satin ribbon, tie knots around button tops and leave decorative ends.

PERSONALIZED PANTS

Your favorite fella' will team these with the Reindeer Sweater to celebrate the holidays in style (Fig. 5-3).

- Cost of materials: $6.00
- Retail cost: $20.00

Materials

Purchased pattern for simple elastic-waist pants
½ yard red Trigger

Fig. 5–3 Personalized pants. Photo by Marnie Leonard.

½ yard ½"-wide white elastic
   (fabric based on toddler's size 3; check pattern instructions for amount
   needed)
Lightweight iron-on interfacing
Scraps of:
   green Trigger
   ⅜" wide red and white striped ribbon
1 gold ⅜" sleigh bell button
Matching threads

Directions

1. Cut out pants according to pattern instructions.
2. Back green Trigger fabric scraps with lightweight iron-on interfacing. Trace letters needed for name from alphabet patterns at end of chapter and cut out from green Trigger.
3. Position and pin letters of name down right leg of pant front. Depending on garment size and length of name, either spread out letters or overlap, as necessary. Appliqué in place, using medium-width zigzag satin stitch.
4. Tie small bow, using red and white striped ribbon, and tack to bottom of vowel in name, with sleigh bell button sewn below bow.
5. Complete pants, following purchased pattern instructions. Press.

Additional Hint

Use the appliqué alphabet to personalize or monogram any of the projects in this book, or any ready-made or handmade items.

REINDEER DUFFLE BAG

You will definitely hear the jingle of sleigh bells with this bell-and-bow trimmed tote (Fig. 5-4) that can carry pajamas for overnight stays with friends or family, or special treasures on a trip to school for "show and tell."

- Cost of materials: $8.50
- Retail cost: $20.00

Materials
½ yard chocolate brown Trigger
¼ yard red mini-dot fabric for lining

Fig. 5–4 Reindeer duffle bag. Photo by Marnie Leonard.

8" brown zipper
Scraps of:
    brown mini-dot fabric
    Thermolam batting
    black acrylic felt
    white acrylic felt
    polyfil stuffing
    double-fold red bias tape
    3/8"-wide green satin ribbon
    5/8"-wide red grosgrain ribbon
2 yards 3/8"-wide red/green/gold holiday striped ribbon
8 brass 1/2" bells
3 brass 1/4" bells
1 brass 3/4" bell
1 red 1" pompom
Hot glue gun and glue sticks
Matching threads

Directions

1. Cut from chocolate brown Trigger: one rectangle 18" × 8½", two duffle ends, two handles 2½" × 22", two ears (one in reverse), eight legs (four in reverse), and one tail.

2. From red mini-dot fabric, cut one lining piece 18" × 8½", and set aside. Fold remaining fabric in half, right sides together. Trace around reindeer antler pattern piece to make two antlers. Pin batting underneath antlers and stitch around drawn lines, leaving end open per pattern piece. Cut out antlers, leaving ¼" seam allowance, clipping curves, and turn right side out. Lightly press. Set antlers aside.

3. From brown mini-dot fabric, cut two ears (one in reverse) and one tail.

4. Pin chocolate brown ears and brown mini-dot ears with right sides together; stitch, using ¼" seam allowance, leaving open per pattern piece. Clip curves and corners and turn right-side-out. Press.

5. Pin chocolate brown tail and brown mini-dot tail together, right sides facing, and stitch using ¼" seam allowance; leave opening as indicated on pattern. Clip curves and turn right-side-out. Lightly stuff and pinch tail so that it stands up a little (Diag. 5-1). Hand hem open end and set aside.

6. Following placement drawing, pinch ears and baste — with brown mini-dot side facing down — to one duffle tote end (Diag. 5-2). Pin and baste antlers over ears and pin antlers to middle of duffle tote end so they will not get caught in duffle end seams. Set aside.

7. Baste zipper along 8½" side of chocolate brown rectangular piece. Pin lin-

ing to duffle rectangle, right sides together, and stitch, using ¼" seam allowance. Turn right-side-out and press. Topstitch ⅛" from edge along zipper.

8. Fold under opposite 8½" side ¼" and press. Baste folded edges to zipper edge (it helps to unzip zipper to do this). Topstitch ⅛" from edge along zipper. Remove basting stitches.

9. Fold two handle pieces in half vertically and stitch, using ¼" seam allowance, leaving open 6" in the middle for turning. Clip corners, turn and hand stitch closed. Press. Stitch red/green/gold holiday striped ribbon lengthwise on each handle piece.

10. Place handles on tote, with ends secured at center bottom. Keep handles 4" apart in the middle. Open zipper and slip duffle on free-arm sewing machine and machine stitch handles ⅛" from edges. If you do not have a free-arm machine, it is much easier to stitch the handles by hand.

11. Pin and baste duffle tote ends to duffle bag. Check to be sure they fit smoothly—if not, take a little tuck at the center bottom of tote. Stitch duffle tote ends with ¼" seam allowance. Encase these seams with double-folded red bias tape for finished edges.

12. Turn duffle right-side-out and unpin end with antlers. Press if necessary. Tie two bows with ⅜"-wide green satin ribbon and tack to inner ear. Tack ¼" brass jingle bells just under bows. Cut 2 eyes from black acrylic felt and glue at jaunty angle to face, following Diag. 5-3. Glue 1" red pompom just under eyes for nose. Tie bow, using ⅝" red grosgrain ribbon, and cut ends in V. Tack bow at chin and sew ¾" brass bell under red bow.

13. Tack tail to opposite end, just after zipper. Tie bow, using holiday striped ribbon, and tack to top of tail. Sew ¼" brass bell by tail bow.

14. With remaining striped ribbon, tie eight bows and cut ends at an angle; set aside. Pin four legs with right sides together and stitch, using ¼" seam allowance; leave opening in each, per pattern. Turn right-side-out, lightly stuff, turn under edges, and lightly gather closed. Tack legs to duffle straps two inches above center bottom. Sew on all four legs in this manner. Tack bows to top of legs to hide stitching (Diag. 5-4). Evenly space and sew two ½" brass bells to each strap side.

BEDTIME BEAR NIGHTSHIRT

On a frosty winter night, your youngsters will love snuggling into warm, cozy nightshirts trimmed with Bedtime Bear appliqués (Fig. 5-5). The special toy teddy (following project) is an added treat. You can appliqué this design to purchased sleepwear or make your own. The nightshirt pictured was sewn, using a simple pattern with just three pieces: front, back, and sleeves. The neck and sleeves are trimmed with white ribbing. The bows and appliqué transform it from plain to pizzazz!

Fig. 5–5 Bedtime Teddy
nightshirt and toy.

■ Cost of materials: $12.50
■ Retail cost: $28.00

Materials

    1 purchased long blue velour nightshirt
    1 yard ⅝"-wide red mini-dot grosgrain ribbon
    1 white ½" pompom
    Scraps of:
        tan velour
        red mini-dot fabric
        white with red heart flower fabric
        tan mini-dot fabric
        brown acrylic felt
    Lightweight iron-on interfacing
    Black embroidery floss
    Pink Venus pencil
    Water-soluble marking pen
    Matching threads

Directions

1. If you are sewing the nightshirt, appliqué design to the upper right section of nightshirt front *before* assembling. If you are using purchased nightshirt, proceed to Step 2.

2. Cut piece of lightweight iron-on interfacing 5" × 8" and fuse to *wrong* side at upper right of nightshirt front. This procedure stabilizes the velour knit, so it does not stretch while appliquéing. Be sure to use a ballpoint sewing machine needle for best results.

3. To appliqué nightshirt, back tan velour, red mini-dot fabric, white with red heart flower print, and tan mini-dot fabric scraps with lightweight iron-on interfacing. Cut out appliqué as follows:

1 nightcap and 1 nightshirt: red mini-dot
1 teddy head, 2 teddy hands, and 1 pair feet: tan velour
1 teddy muzzle: tan mini-dot
1 teddy nose: brown acrylic felt
1 glass and 1 cookie: white with red heart flower print

4. Trace topstitching lines on appliqués for nightshirt, nightcap, and glass, using water-soluble marking pen. Cut slit in nightcap for right ear and cut slits in teddy nightshirt for hands.

5. Position and pin teddy bear with right ear tucked *out* on right side of nightcap. Appliqué cap in place with medium-width zigzag satin stitch. Pin and position nightshirt, with teddy hands tucked in nightshirt sleeves. Tuck glass of milk appliqué into left hand and cookie into right hand. Appliqué design in the following order, using medium-width zigzag satin stitch: teddy head, nightshirt, and feet. Using narrow-width zigzag satin stitch, appliqué muzzle, hands, glass, and cookie.

6. Topstitch details on nightshirt and nightcap, using white thread and straight machine stitch. Tack nose to muzzle and embroider mouth in back stitch, using two strands of black floss. Embroider eyes in satin stitch, using two strands black floss. Hand embroider buttons on nightshirt in satin stitch, using gold metallic thread. Tack white ½" pompom to end of nightcap. Lightly shade cheeks and inner ears with pink Venus pencil.

7. Tie three bows, using ⅝"-wide red mini-dot grosgrain ribbon, cutting ends in V. Tack one bow to left front neckline, just below ribbing, and other two bows on each side of nightshirt slits at bottom.

8. If making nightshirt for boy, omit bows and substitute ¾" red star buttons.

BEDTIME BEAR TOY

An adorable teddy to complement the nightshirt, also shown in Fig. 5-5.

- Cost of materials: $4.00
- Retail cost: $10.00

Materials

⅛ yard tan velour (will make 4 bears)
⅛ yard red solid knit fabric
Polyfil stuffing
Scraps of:
    red mini-dot fabric
    brown acrylic felt
    tan acrylic felt
    white with red heart flower print fabric
    ⅛"-wide gold metallic ribbon
1 light blue teddy bear face button
1 white ½" pompom
Black fine-line Sharpie marker
Pink Venus pencil
Hot glue gun and glue sticks
Matching threads, including gold metallic thread

Directions

1. Trace bear pattern onto wrong side of tan velour. Fold velour with right sides together, and stitch on drawn line, leaving open on left outer leg. Cut out bear, allowing ⅛" seam allowance. Turn right-side-out, stuff, and hand stitch closed. Cut out muzzle from tan velour and use a hand running stitch around outer edge of muzzle. Put tiny amount of polyfil stuffing in center of muzzle, and pull stitching tightly. Knot securely. Glue muzzle to bear face, as shown.

2. Cut out nose from brown acrylic felt and glue in place. Using double thread, stitch from eye to eye, pulling slightly to indent eyes a little and give a bridge to the nose above the muzzle. Cut two eyes from brown acrylic felt and glue in place. Draw in eyelashes, eyebrows, and mouth, using black fine-line Sharpie marker. With double thread, work running stitch around neck and pull slightly to give neck a little shape. Lightly shade inner ears and cheeks with pink Venus pencil.

3. Cut nightcap and nightshirt from red solid knit fabric, per pattern pieces. Stitch around nightcap, using ⅛" seam allowance, with right sides together, leaving open for head per pattern piece. Turn right-side-out, lightly stuff end of cap, and slit places for ears. Fit cap on bear head, pulling ears through slits. Tuck under raw edges around ears. Turn under edge of cap around bear face ⅛"; hand stitch to bear head, using gold metallic thread. Tie bow, using ⅛"-wide gold metallic ribbon, and tack to lower right ear. Glue pompom to end of nightcap.

4. With right sides together, stitch shoulder, underarm, and side seams of nightshirt, using ⅛" seam allowance. Clip curves, turn, and put on bear. Turn under sleeve ends ⅛" and hand stitch to bear, using gold metallic thread. Turn un-

der fabric around V-neck ⅛″ and hand stitch to bear, using gold metallic thread. Hand topstitch detail to nightshirt front per pattern, using gold metallic thread. Using red thread, hand stitch hem of bear's nightshirt, using ⅛″ seam allowance.

5. Cut a 4″ square of red mini-dot fabric and hem all edges with ⅛″ seam allowance. Cut heart from white with red print fabric and appliqué to one of the corners, as shown in Fig. 5-5. Fold into quarters and, ½″ from folded corner, wrap thread around corner and pull to make a little puff at the top. Knot securely. At the ½″ mark, tack blanket to bear's left hand and sew bear button to cover stitching.

6. Cut a cookie from tan acrylic felt and chocolate chips from brown acrylic felt. Glue chips to cookie and cookie to right hand of bear. Fold right arm in toward bear body and tack in place.

Variations

- If making this bear for a child under the age of three, omit bow at right inner ear, cookie in right hand, and button on blanket. Be sure to stitch blanket to left hand very securely and, in addition to gluing muzzle to bear head, hand stitch it as well. Omit brown acrylic bear nose and embroider one instead, using brown embroidery floss. Embroider eyes using brown embroidery floss.
- This bear can be dressed in any style you prefer. Let your child choose the outfits for a whole wardrobe of bear duds! Make some to match the clothing projects in this book: They will be treasured.

TEDDY BEAR CHRISTMAS STOCKINGS

Make several of these charming stockings (shown in Fig. 5-6) and vary details slightly to best suit each family member. These stockings are a wonderful way to use bits and pieces of scraps and ribbon trims to excellent advantage.

- Cost of materials: $8.50
- Retail cost: $25.00

Materials for Girl's Stocking
½ yard quilted Christmas green mini-print fabric (will make two stockings)
¼ yard ¾″-wide red/green striped grosgrain ribbon
¼ yard 2″-wide gathered eyelet lace
1 yard ⅝″-wide white satin picot ribbon
1 yard ⅜″-wide red satin picot ribbon
Scraps of:
   tan velour
   red mini-dot fabric
   tan mini-floral print fabric
   black acrylic felt
   red and white mini-striped fabric

Fig. 5–6 Girl's and boy's
teddy Christmas stockings.

white with red heart flower print
eyelet lace insert
eyelet lace trim
white scallop lace trim
red single-fold bias tape
1/8"-wide red mini-dot satin ribbon
1/8"-wide red satin ribbon
3/8"-wide red and white mini-striped ribbon
1/8"-wide green satin ribbon
Thermolam batting
polyfil stuffing
2–6mm brown animal eyes
1 green 1/2" heart button
1 red 1/4" heart button
1 doll button
1 white mouse button
2 tan 3/4" pompoms
2 tan 1/2" pompoms
Lightweight iron-on interfacing
Black fine-line Sharpie marker
Pink Venus pencil

Hot glue gun and glue sticks
Matching threads

Directions

1. Join pattern pieces supplied at end of chapter; cut 2 stockings (1 in reverse) from quilted Christmas green print fabric.

2. Sew 2"-wide eyelet lace trim 2" from top of stocking. Pin red/green striped grosgrain ribbon trim so bottom edge is over binding of eyelet lace. Stitch in place along top and bottom edges of ribbon. Trim any excess lace and ribbon from ends.

3. Back red mini-dot, red and white mini-stripe, and white with red heart flower print fabric scraps with lightweight iron-on interfacing. Cut out appliqué pieces as follows:

1 right sleeve, 1 left sleeve, 1 nightgown, and Christmas package: red mini-dot fabric
1 nightgown bodice: eyelet lace insert
1 Christmas package: red and white mini-stripe
1 Christmas package: white with red print

4. To make teddy bear head, trace bear face on wrong side of tan velour. Fold velour with right sides together and place double thickness of Thermolam batting underneath, stitching on traced line. Cut out face, leaving 1/8" seam allowance. Cut a slit in back of head, being careful not to cut through more than one layer, and turn right-side-out. Hand stitch closed. Take a little tuck stitch under each inner ear and pull thread to indent ear a little. Lightly shade inner ear, using pink Venus pencil.

5. Cut muzzle from tan mini-floral print and use a hand running stitch around outer edge of muzzle. Put tiny amount of polyfil stuffing in center of muzzle and pull stitching tightly. Knot securely. Glue muzzle to face, per pattern. Cut out nose from black acrylic felt and glue in place. Stitch eyes per pattern, pulling tightly to indent area a little. Glue brown animal eyes in eye indentations. Using black Sharpie fine-line marker, draw in eyelashes, eyebrows, and mouth to smile. Cut two tiny heart cheeks from red mini-dot fabric and glue in place.

6. Position and pin nightgown and eyelet lace bodice on lower center of stocking; appliqué with medium-width zigzag satin stitch. Position and pin sleeves on sides of nightgown and appliqué with narrow zigzag satin stitch.

7. Arrange Christmas packages, slightly overlapping, on stocking toe; appliqué, using medium-width zigzag satin stitch. Trim Christmas packages with snips of lace and tiny bows. Sew white mouse button to right of packages, as in photograph.

8. Tack eyelet lace trim under bear head to make a lace collar, turning under ends. Glue teddy head to stocking above nightgown. Tie bow, using 1/8"-wide red

mini-dot satin ribbon, and glue under chin. Tie bow, using ⅛"-wide red satin ribbon, and glue to bottom of right inner ear. Sew ¼" red heart button to center of lace insert. Trim sleeves and nightgown hem with scallop lace trim. Sew doll button to right sleeve end. Glue ½" tan pompoms to sleeve ends for hands. Glue ¾" tan pompoms to nightgown bottom for feet.

9. Pin stocking with right sides together; stitch, using ¼" seam allowance, 4" down right side. Open stocking and sew red bias tape along right side top edge. Turn bias tape to wrong side of stocking and hand hem tape in place. With right sides together, pin rest of stocking and continue stitching with ¼" seam allowance. Turn stocking right side out and press lightly.

10. Layer white and red picot ribbons, with white ribbon on bottom. Make a six-loop bow and tack in center. Tack bow to top right stocking edge. Sew green heart button to center of bow. Make ribbon loop and stitch ends to wrong side of stocking along side bow for stocking hanger.

Materials for Boy's Stocking
   ½ yard quilted Christmas green mini-print fabric (will make two stockings)
   ¼ yard ¾"-wide red/green striped grosgrain ribbon
   ¼ yard 2"-wide gathered eyelet lace
   ⅓ yard ⅝"-wide Christmas green grosgrain ribbon
   ⅓ yard ⅜"-wide white/red mini-striped grosgrain ribbon
   Scraps of:
      tan velour
      red mini-dot fabric
      tan mini-floral print fabric
      black acrylic felt
      red and white mini-striped fabric
      white with red heart flower print
      red single-fold bias tape
      red sweatshirt fleece knit
      ⅛"-wide red mini-dot satin ribbon
      ⅛"-wide red satin ribbon
      ⅛"-wide green satin ribbon
      Thermolam batting
      polyfil stuffing
   2–6mm brown animal eyes
   1 red bell trimmer button
   3 tiny white beads
   1 teddy bear button
   1 white mouse button
   2 tan ¾" pompoms
   2 tan ½" pompoms

1 white ½" pompom
Lightweight iron-on interfacing
Black fine-line Sharpie marker
Pink Venus pencil
Hot glue gun and glue sticks
Matching threads

Directions

1. Join pattern pieces supplied for stockings; cut out stockings (1 in reverse) from quilted green fabric.

2. Sew 2"-wide eyelet lace trim 2" from top of stocking. Pin red/green striped grosgrain ribbon trim so bottom edge is over binding of eyelet lace. Stitch in place along top and bottom edges of ribbon. Trim any excess lace and ribbon from ends.

3. Back red mini-dot, red and white mini-stripe, and white with red heart flower print fabric scraps with lightweight iron-on interfacing. Cut out appliqué pieces as follows:

   1 right sleeve, 1 left sleeve, 1 nightshirt, and 1 Christmas package: red and white mini-stripe
   1 nightshirt collar and 1 Christmas package: red mini-dot
   1 Christmas package: white with red print

4. To make teddy bear head, trace bear face on wrong side of tan velour. Fold velour with right sides together and place double thickness of Thermolam batting underneath; stitch on traced line. Cut out face, leaving ⅛" seam allowance. Cut a slit in back of head, being careful not to cut through more than one layer, and turn right-side-out. Hand stitch closed. Take a little tuck stitch under each inner ear and pull thread to indent ear a little. Lightly shade inner ear using pink Venus pencil.

5. Cut muzzle from tan mini-floral print and work a running stitch around outer edge of muzzle. Put tiny amount of polyfil stuffing in center of muzzle and pull stitching tightly. Knot securely. Glue muzzle to face, per pattern. Cut out nose from black acrylic felt and glue in place. Stitch eyes per pattern, pulling tightly to indent area a little. Glue brown animal eyes in eye indentations. Using black Sharpie fine-line marker, draw in eyelashes, eyebrows and smile. Cut two tiny heart cheeks from red mini-dot fabric and glue in place. Fold piece of red sweatshirt fleece with right sides together and trace around nightcap. Stitch along traced line, leaving cap open per pattern. Turn right side out, lightly stuff with polyfil stuffing, and cut slits for ears. Fit nightcap on bear head and glue in place on head. Glue white pompom to nightcap tip.

6. Position and pin nightshirt to lower center of stocking; appliqué, using me-

dium-width zigzag satin stitch. Position nightshirt collar and appliqué with narrow zigzag satin stitch. Position and pin sleeves on sides of nightshirt and appliqué with narrow zigzag satin stitch.

7. Arrange Christmas packages, slightly overlapping, on stocking toe; appliqué, using medium-width zigzag satin stitch. Trim Christmas packages with snips of lace, tiny bows, and buttons. Sew white mouse button to right of packages, as shown in Fig. 5-6.

8. Glue teddy head to stocking above nightshirt. Glue three white beads down button placket as buttons. Sew teddy button to right sleeve end. Glue ½" tan pompoms to sleeve ends for hands. Glue ¾" tan pompoms to nightshirt bottom for feet.

9. Pin stocking with right sides together; stitch, using ¼" seam allowance, 4" down right side. Open stocking and sew red bias tape along right side top edge. Turn bias tape to wrong side of stocking and hand hem tape in place. With right sides together, pin rest of stocking and continue stitching with ¼" seam allowance. Turn stocking right-side-out and press lightly.

10. Make two-loop bow, using ⅝"-wide Christmas green grosgrain ribbon, and tack in center. Cut ribbon ends in V. With ⅜"-wide red and white mini-striped ribbon, make small six-loop bow and tack in center. Tack both bows together and sew red bell trimmer button to center of bow. Tack bow to top right stocking edge. Make ribbon loop and stitch ends to wrong side of stocking alongside bow for stocking hanger.

SUNBONNET ANGEL PINAFORE

The classical elegance of white-on-white lace appliqué always reminds me of an era of grace and gentility, high tea on the front lawn, and the charm of a Victorian table setting. The Sunbonnet Angel Pinafore shown in the color section recaptures that graceful style—yet adds a hint of today with easy machine appliqué and modern wash-and-wear eyelet lace. Versatile enough to be worn over velvet party dresses for the holiday season, or as a fresh sundress for a special summer occasion, it can also be made full-length for weddings or other formal occasions.

Choose a simple pinafore pattern with a square neckline, ruffled sleeves, and gathered skirt. The pattern I used for this project has only four pattern pieces: bodice, sleeve ruffle, waistband, and skirt. This is an excellent excuse to dig into your lace and eyelet scrap bags and use them most creatively.

- Cost of materials: $10.00
- Retail cost: $45.00

Materials

Purchased pinafore pattern
1½ yards white eyelet fabric, heavily embroidered on bottom edge
1 yard ¾"-wide white diamond-edge lace trim

2 yards ⅝"-wide white eyelet ribbon
(based on child's size 4; check pattern instructions for fabric amounts)
¼ yard tear-away interfacing
¼ yard 4"-wide white flat eyelet lace, with scallop on top and bottom edges
Scraps of:
white piqué
white eyelet lace trims
white scallop lace trims
¼"-wide white satin ribbon
lightweight iron-on interfacing
White thread

Directions

1. Cut out pinafore from eyelet fabric, using heavily embroidered bottom edge for skirt hem. Check your pattern pieces when buying fabric to be sure that you have enough border.

2. Back white piqué with lightweight iron-on interfacing. Cut out appliqué wings, pinafore, and sleeve, using the natural edges of the 4"-wide white flat eyelet lace with scallop edges to guide the shape as much as possible. Cut out appliqué pieces as follows:

1 sunbonnet body, 1 hat brim, and 1 pair feet: white piqué
1 angel pinafore, 2 wings, 1 arm, and 1 hat back: eyelet scallop lace

3. To position appliqué, place tear-away interfacing under bodice to stabilize eyelet fabrics and layer appliqué, following placement drawing. Using narrow zigzag satin stitch, appliqué the pieces in the following order: sunbonnet body, sunbonnet feet, sunbonnet pinafore, sunbonnet wings, hat brim, hat back, and arm. Trim edge of hat brim with scallop lace and trim sunbonnet skirt bottom with white diamond-edge lace trim. Tie bow, using ¼"-wide white satin ribbon, and tack to back of sunbonnet skirt just under bottom wing. Lightly press and remove tear-away interfacing from appliqué.

4. Trim neckline with white diamond-edge lace trim and assemble pinafore, following pattern instructions.

5. Baste ⅝"-wide white eyelet ribbon down center of waistband and sew on both edges. Repeat for back waistband. Press pinafore, using spray starch for extra crispness.

CHRISTMAS GOOSE SWEATER

A charming Christmas goose adorns the sweater in Fig. 5-7, suitable for either a boy or girl.

- Cost of material: $12.00
- Retail cost: $25.00

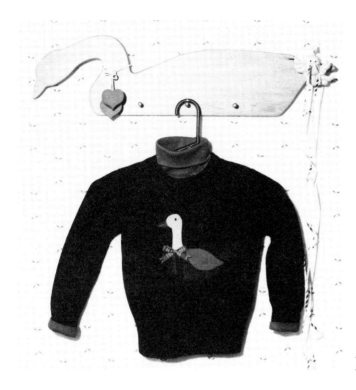

Fig. 5–7 Christmas Goose
Sweater.

Materials

Purchased hunter green acrylic crewneck sweater
Lightweight iron-on interfacing
Scraps of:
 red plaid fabric
 tan with navy mini-dot fabric
 red mini-dot fabric
 blue/green/red plaid fabric
Navy blue embroidery floss
¼ yard ⅜″-wide red plaid ribbon
Matching threads

Directions

1. Cut piece of lightweight iron-on interfacing 7½″ × 7½″ and fuse to wrong side at center sweater front. This procedure stabilizes the sweater knit so it doesn't stretch while appliquéing. Be sure to use a ballpoint sewing machine needle for best results.

2. Back red plaid fabric, tan with navy mini-dot fabric, red mini-dot fabric,

and blue/green/red plaid fabric scraps with lightweight iron-on interfacing. Cut out appliqué pieces as follows:

1 beak: red plaid
1 goose head/neck: tan with navy mini-dot
1 wing: red mini-dot
1 body: navy/green/red plaid

3. Position, pin, and appliqué pieces in the following order using medium-width zigzag satin stitch: goose beak, goose head/neck, goose body, and goose wing. Using two strands navy blue embroidery floss, satin stitch eye.

4. Tie bow, using red plaid ribbon, cutting ends in V. Tack to left side of goose neck where it meets the body. Using pressing cloth, lightly steam press the appliqué.

Stocking Stuffers

I sometimes feel that there is a naughty little elf who sets the speed of all the clocks to double-time in the month of December. There never seems to be enough time to trim the tree, deck the halls and finish all of the Christmas presents that are on my list. By adding special touches to ready-made staples such as hats, mittens and gloves, you can finish projects in a jiffy, still knowing that you added that extra bit of love to each item

REINDEER HAT AND MITTEN SET

A delightful Christmas surprise, this set (Fig. 5-8) can be made in a jiffy.

- Cost of materials: $10.00
- Retail cost: $27.50

Materials

1 purchased navy blue knit ski cap
1 purchased pair red knit mittens
1 package white snowflake sequins
Scraps of:
  tan velour
  Thermolam batting
  yellow mini-floral print
  tan mini-floral print
  lightweight iron-on interfacing
  Stitch Witchery
  red mini-dot fabric
  ⅛"-wide red picot ribbon
  ⅜"-wide red plaid ribbon
3 brass ¼" bells
6 brown animal eyes, 6mm diameter

Fig. 5–8 Reindeer hat and mittens. Photo by Marnie Leonard.

Brown fine-line Sharpie marker
Pink Venus pencil
Hot glue gun and glue sticks
Matching threads

Directions

1. Make three reindeer heads in the following manner: trace reindeer face on wrong side of tan velour. Fold velour, with right sides together, and place double thickness of Thermolam batting underneath, stitching on traced line. Cut out face, leaving ⅛" seam allowance. Cut a slit in the back of the head, being careful not to cut through more than one layer, and turn right-side-out. Hand stitch closed. Fuse lightweight iron-on interfacing to back of tan mini-floral print fabric; cut muzzle out and glue to lower face, per pattern. Cut out nose from red mini-dot and glue to muzzle. Stitch eyes, pulling tightly to indent area a little. Glue brown animal eyes in eye indentations. Using brown Sharpie fine-line marker, draw in eyelashes, eyebrows, and smiling mouth. Lightly shade inner ears and cheeks with pink Venus pencil.

2. With wrong sides together, fuse pieces of yellow mini-floral print so you have a single reversible piece. Cut out antlers and finish edges with medium-width zigzag satin stitch. Glue antlers to back of reindeer head. Tie bow, using ⅛"-wide red picot ribbon, and tack to bottom of right ear. Tie bow, using ⅜" red plaid ribbon, and tack to chin. Sew ¼" brass bell under bow.

3. Glue finished reindeer head to ribbing of ski cap with antlers placed just over edge of hat cuff. Glue eight white snowflake sequins to hat in random fashion, scattering them like falling snow.

4. Glue completed reindeer heads to top of mitten hands. Glue five white snowflake sequins to each mitten in random fashion, scattering them like falling snow.

TEDDY TRIMMED GLOVES AND SCARF

Another sure-to-please stocking stuffer (Fig. 5-9).

- Cost of materials: $10.00
- Retail cost: $20.00

Materials

1 purchased pair bright green gloves
⅙ yard navy and red plaid washable wool, 54"–60" wide
1 package white snowflake sequins
Scraps of:
    tan velour
    Thermolam batting
    polyfil stuffing
    tan mini-floral print

Fig. 5–9 Teddy gloves and scarf set. Photo by Marnie Leonard.

120

lightweight iron-on interfacing
red mini-dot fabric
⅛"-wide red satin ribbon
⅜"-wide red plaid ribbon
black acrylic felt
3 brass ¼" bells
6 brown animal eyes, 6mm diameter
Black fine-line Sharpie marker
Pink Venus pencil
Hot glue gun and glue sticks
Matching threads

Directions

1. To make scarf, hem side seams with ¼" seam allowance and press.

2. Make three teddy bear heads in the following manner: trace bear face on wrong side of tan velour. Fold velour with right sides together and place double thickness of Thermolam batting underneath, stitching on traced line. Cut out face, leaving ⅛" seam allowance. Cut a slit in back of head, being careful not to cut through more than one layer; turn right-side-out. Hand stitch closed. Take a little tuck stitch under each inner ear and pull thread to indent ear a little. Lightly shade inner ear, using pink Venus pencil.

3. Cut muzzle from tan mini-floral print and work hand running stitch around outer edge of muzzle. Put tiny amount of polyfil stuffing in center of muzzle and pull stitching tightly. Knot securely. Glue muzzle to face, per pattern. Cut out nose from black acrylic felt and glue in place. Stitch eyes, per pattern, pulling tightly to indent area a little. Glue brown animal eyes in eye indentations. Using black Sharpie fine-line marker, draw in eyelashes, eyebrows, and smiling mouth. Cut two tiny heart cheeks from red mini-dot fabric and glue in place.

4. Tie ⅛"-wide red satin ribbon in tiny bow and glue to bottom of right inner ear. Tie bow, using ⅜" red plaid ribbon, and tack under chin. Glue ¼" brass bell under bow.

5. For gloves, glue teddy head to top of glove hand and glue five white snowflake sequins to each glove in random fashion, scattering them like falling snow.

6. Glue teddy head to end of scarf in center, 2½" from end. Glue seven white snowflake sequins to scarf end in random fashion, scattering them like falling snow.

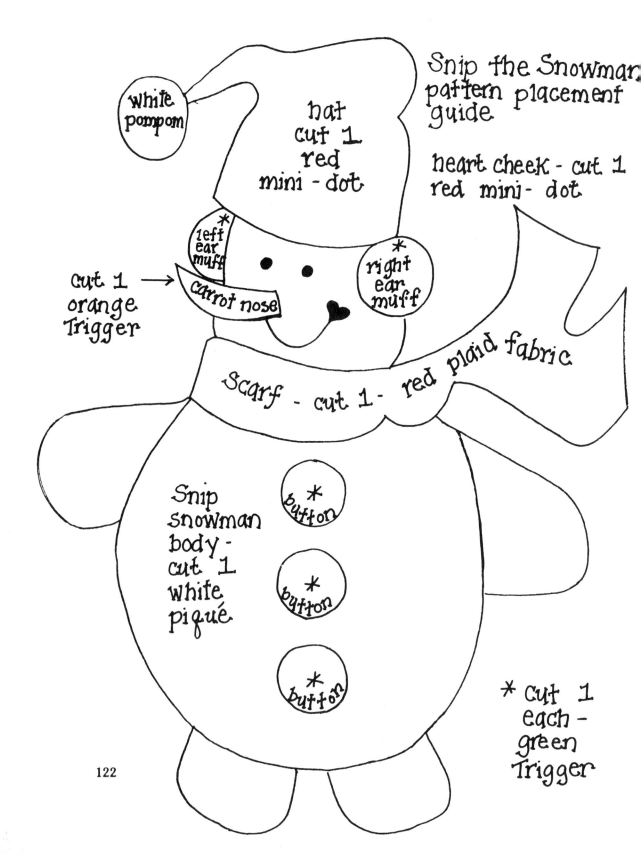

white pompom

Snip the Snowman pattern placement guide

hat cut 1 red mini - dot

heart cheek - cut 1 red mini - dot

*left ear muff

*right ear muff

cut 1 orange Trigger

carrot nose

Scarf - cut 1 - red plaid fabric

Snip snowman body - cut 1 white piqué

*button

*button

*button

* cut 1 each - green Trigger

Snip the Snowman Appliqué Pattern

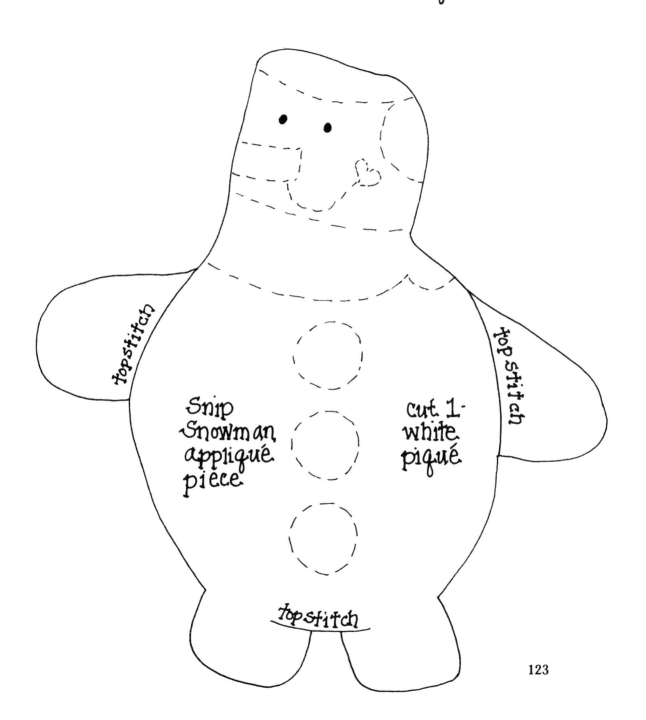

topstitch

topstitch

Snip
Snowman
appliqué
piece

cut 1
white
piqué

topstitch

123

Snip the Snowman
Appliqué Patterns

heart
cheek
cut 1 →
♡

left
ear
muff
cut
1

carrot nose
cut 1
orange Trigger

red
mini-
dot

right
ear
muff
cut 1

snowman
cap
cut 1
red
mini — dot

cut 3
buttons

* green
Trigger

scarf - cut 1 - red plaid fabric

holly leaf
pattern - cut 2
green
acrylic
felt

X - holly
placement
on cap

X

small
version
of
Snip
appliqué

124

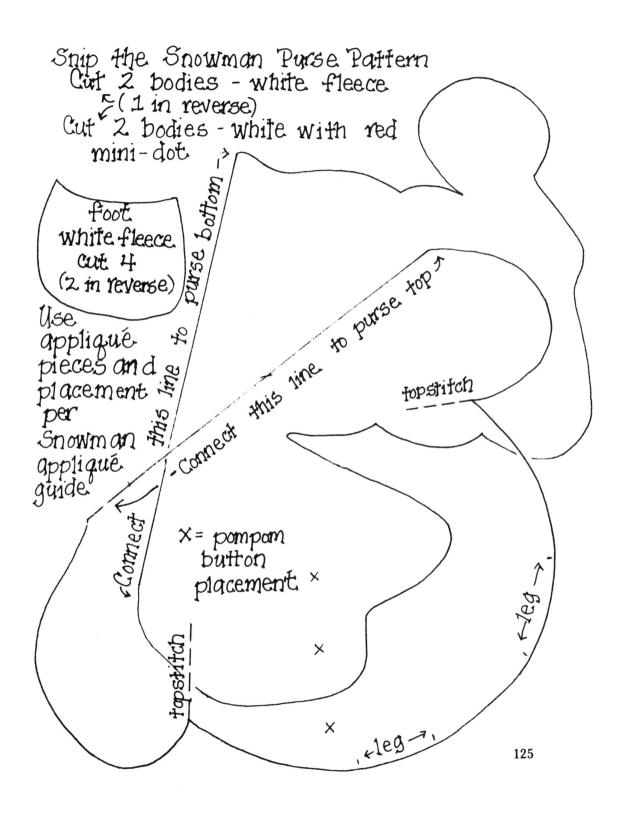

Snip the Snowman Purse Pattern
Cut 2 bodies - white fleece
(1 in reverse)
Cut 2 bodies - white with red
mini-dot

foot
white fleece
cut 4
(2 in reverse)

Use
appliqué
pieces and
placement
per
Snowman
appliqué
guide.

Connect this line to purse bottom →

Connect this line to purse top ↗

Connect →

← Connect

topstitch

topstitch

X = pompom
button
placement ×

×

×

← leg →

← leg →

125

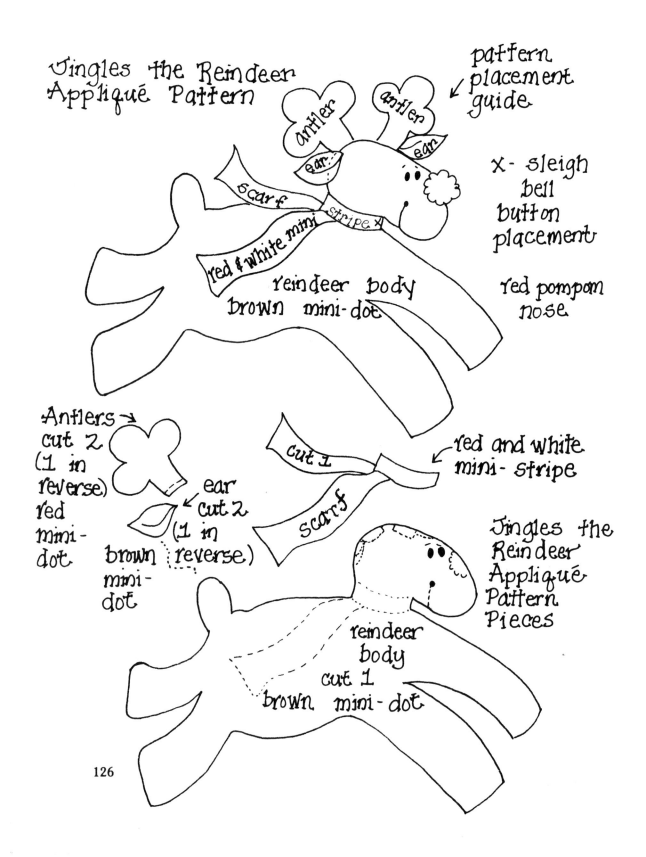

Jingles the Reindeer
Appliqué Pattern

pattern
placement
guide

antler

antler

ear

ear

scarf

stripe X

red & white mini

reindeer body
brown mini-dot

X- sleigh
bell
button
placement

red pompom
nose.

Antlers →
cut 2
(1 in
reverse)
red
mini-
dot.

ear
cut 2
(1 in
reverse)
brown
mini-
dot

cut 1

scarf

red and white
mini- stripe

Jingles the
Reindeer
Appliqué
Pattern
Pieces

reindeer
body
cut 1
brown mini-dot

126

Appliqué Alphabet

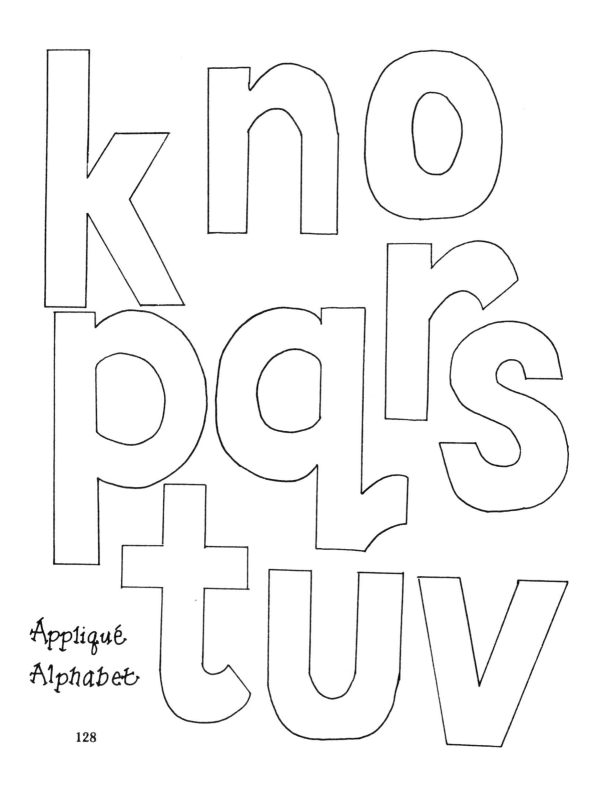

knopqrstuv

Appliqué
Alphabet

128

WXYZ

← leave open →

Reindeer
tote bag ear
Cut 2 - brown Trigger
(1 in reverse)
cut 2 - brown mini-
dot

↑ Appliqué Alphabet

Reindeer tote bag antler

red mini - dot fabric

← leave open →

129

Pattern pieces · Jingles Reindeer Duffle Tote Bag

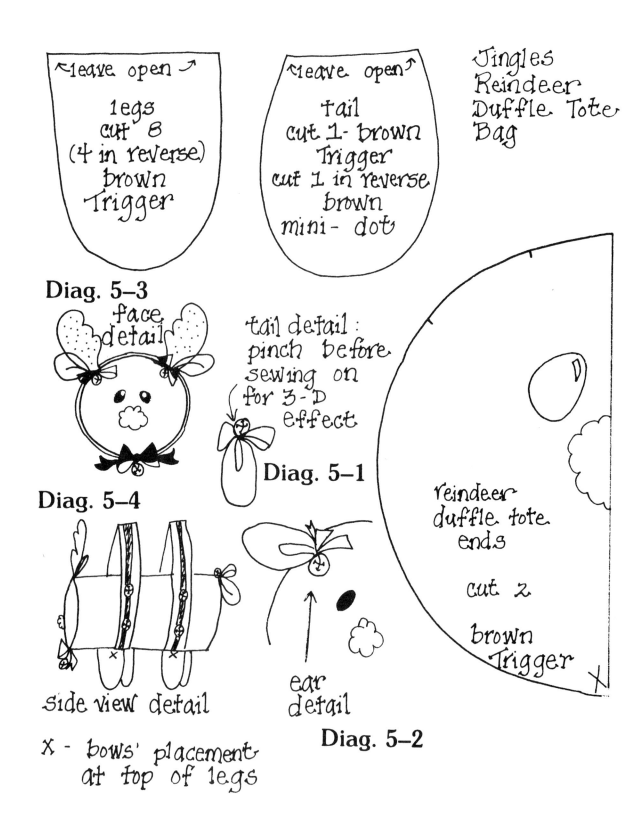

~leave open↗

legs
cut 8
(4 in reverse)
brown
Trigger

~leave open↗

tail
cut 1- brown
Trigger
cut 1 in reverse
brown
mini- dot

Jingles
Reindeer
Duffle Tote
Bag

Diag. 5–3

face
detail

tail detail:
pinch before
sewing on
for 3-D
effect

Diag. 5–1

Diag. 5–4

reindeer
duffle tote
ends

cut 2

brown
Trigger

side view detail

ear
detail

Diag. 5–2

X - bows' placement
at top of legs

Placement pattern

nightcap
cut 1
topstitch   slit
red mini-dot

BB

head

left hand *

rt. hand *

cut 1 tan mini-dot

muzzle

feet   *

* cut 1 each tan velour

glass
cut 1 each white with red heart flower print

cookie

nose-cut 1- brown acrylic felt

Bedtime Bear Appliqué Pattern

topstitch

Nightshirt cut 1 red mini-dot

slit

slit

BB

131

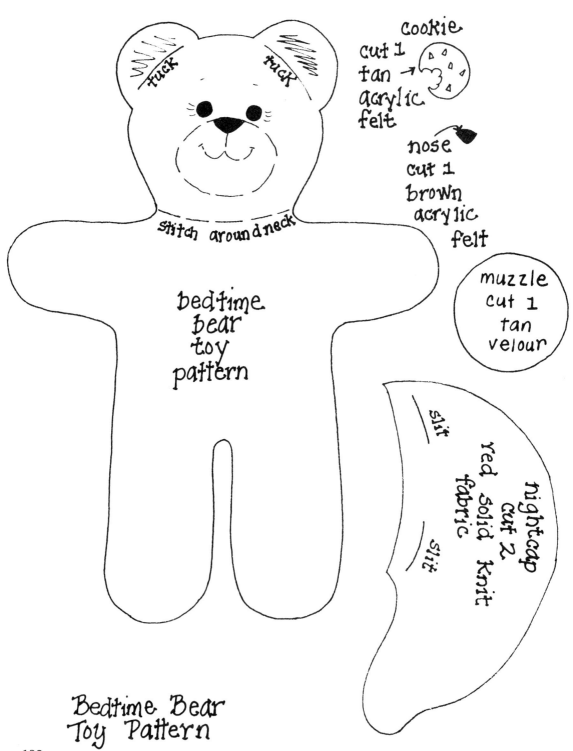

cookie
cut 1
tan
acrylic
felt

nose
cut 1
brown
acrylic
felt

muzzle
cut 1
tan
velour

tuck   tuck

stitch around neck

bedtime
bear
toy
pattern

nightcap
cut 2
red solid knit
fabric

slit

slit

Bedtime Bear
Toy Pattern

Bedtime Bear Toy Pattern

neck back

topstitching detail

nightshirt
cut 1 with regular neck and
cut 1 with "V" neck

red solid knit fabric

note topstitching detail

Teddy Bear

Head Pattern

for Christmas

Stockings and

for Stocking

Stuffers

tuck   tuck

muzzle tan mini-floral

cut 1 per teddy head

nose · cut 1 per teddy head · black acrylic felt

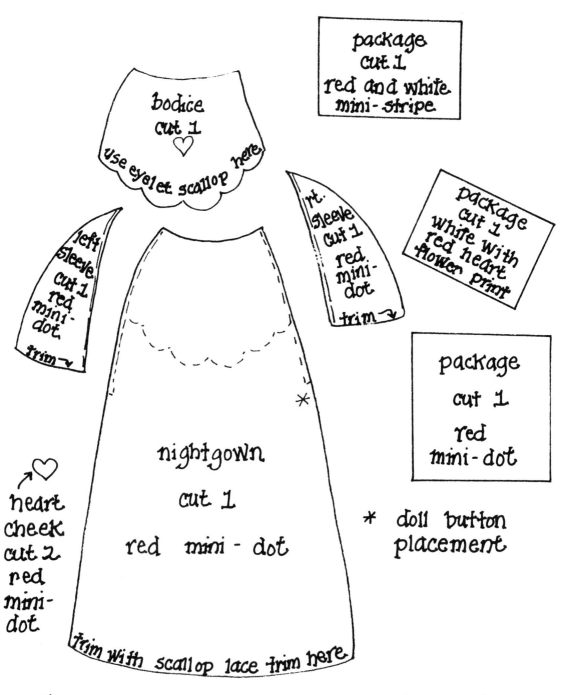

package
cut 1
red and white
mini-stripe

package
cut 1
white with
red heart
flower print

package
cut 1
red
mini-dot

bodice
cut 1
♡
use eyelet scallop here

rt.
sleeve
cut 1
red
mini-
dot
trim→

left
sleeve
cut 1
red
mini-
dot
trim→

nightgown

cut 1

red mini-dot

→♡
heart
cheek
cut 2
red
mini-
dot

* doll button
placement

trim with scallop lace trim here

Girl's Teddy Bear Christmas Stocking Appliqué
Pattern

134

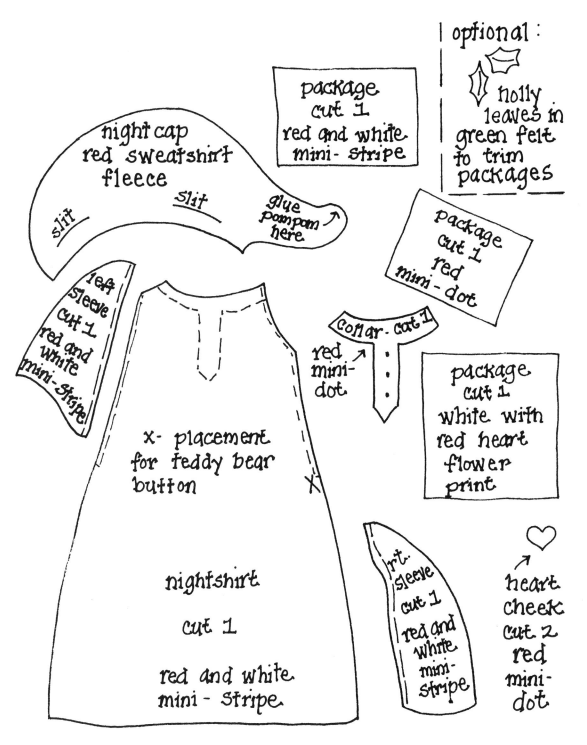

optional:
holly leaves in green felt to trim packages

package cut 1 red and white mini-stripe

night cap red sweatshirt fleece

slit

slit

glue pompom here

package cut 1 red mini-dot

left sleeve cut 1 red and white mini-stripe

collar cut 1

red mini-dot

x- placement for teddy bear button

package cut 1 white with red heart flower print

X

nightshirt

cut 1

red and white mini-stripe

rt. sleeve cut 1 red and white mini-stripe

heart cheek cut 2 red mini-dot

Boy's Teddy Bear Christmas Stocking Pattern Pieces

Teddy Bear Christmas Stockings

trim with eyelet lace and ribbon
along this line ⌣

← Connect to stocking bottom here ⌣

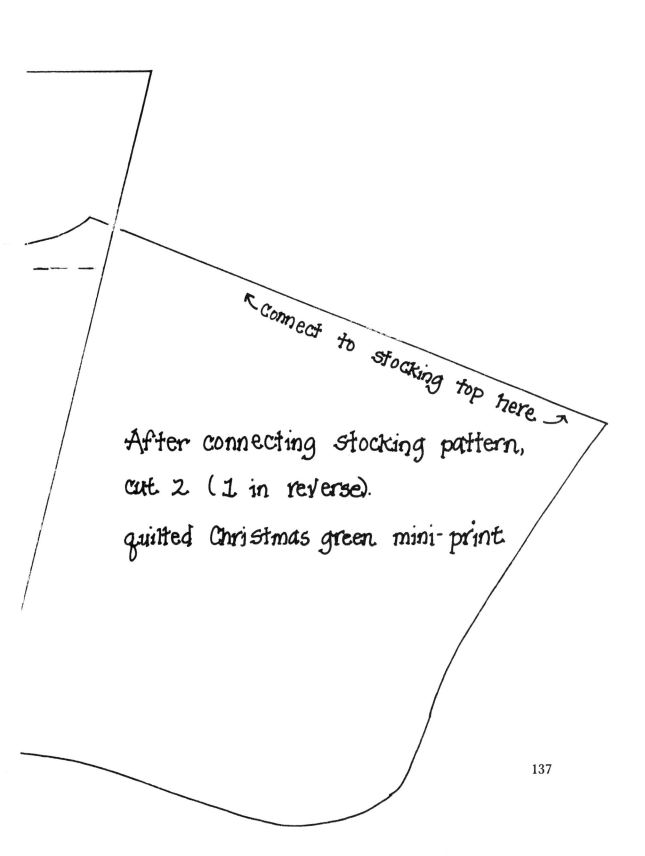

← Connect to stocking top here. ↗

After connecting stocking pattern,
cut 2 (1 in reverse).
quilted Christmas green mini-print

137

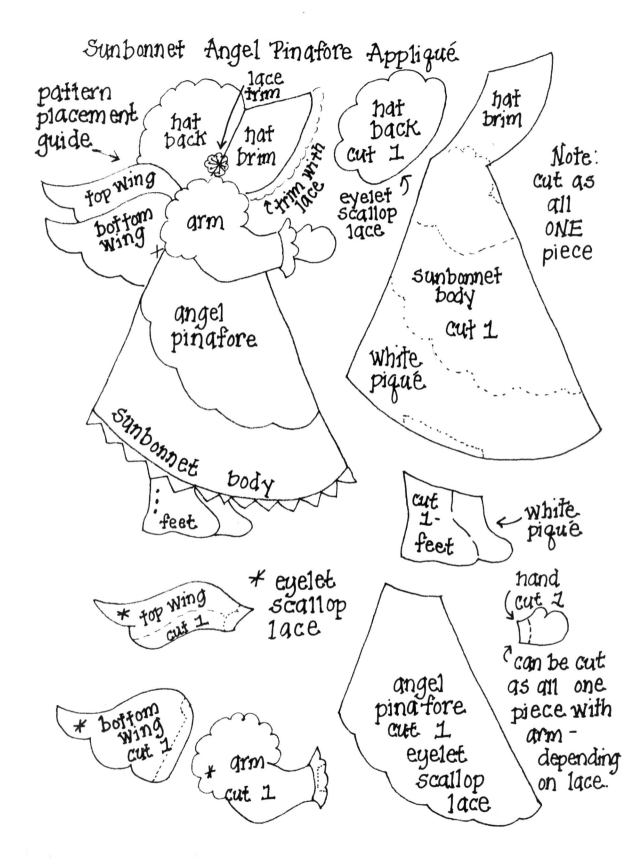

Sunbonnet Angel Pinafore Appliqué

pattern placement guide

lace trim

hat back

hat brim

top wing

bottom wing

arm

← trim with lace

hat back cut 1

eyelet scallop lace

hat brim

Note: cut as all ONE piece

sunbonnet body cut 1

white piqué

angel pinafore

sunbonnet body

feet

cut 1 - feet

← white piqué

hand cut 2

↰ can be cut as all one piece with arm - depending on lace.

* top wing cut 1

* eyelet scallop lace

* bottom wing cut 1

* arm cut 1

angel pinafore cut 1 eyelet scallop lace

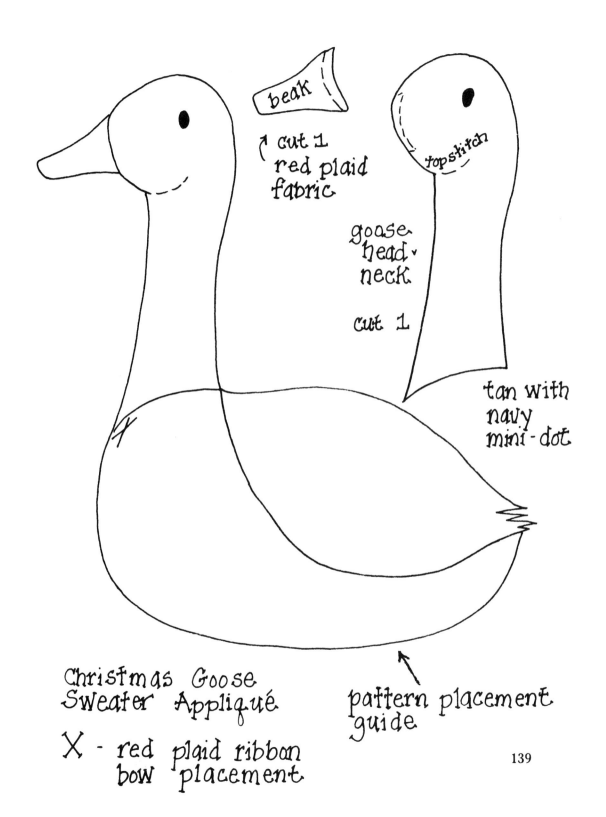

beak

cut 1
red plaid
fabric

goose
head·
neck

cut 1

topstitch

tan with
navy
mini-dot

Christmas Goose
Sweater Appliqué

X - red plaid ribbon
    bow placement

pattern placement
guide

139

Christmas Goose Sweater Appliqué Pattern

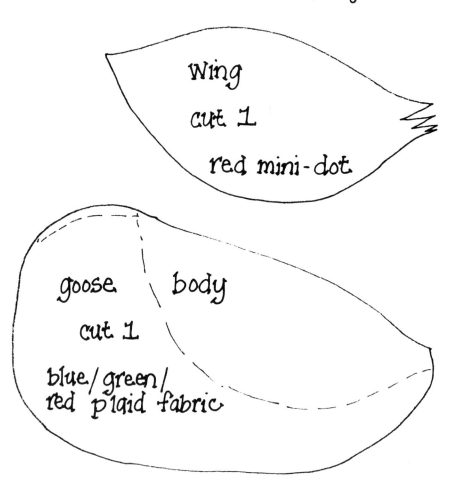

Wing

cut 1

red mini-dot

goose body

cut 1

blue/green/
red plaid fabric

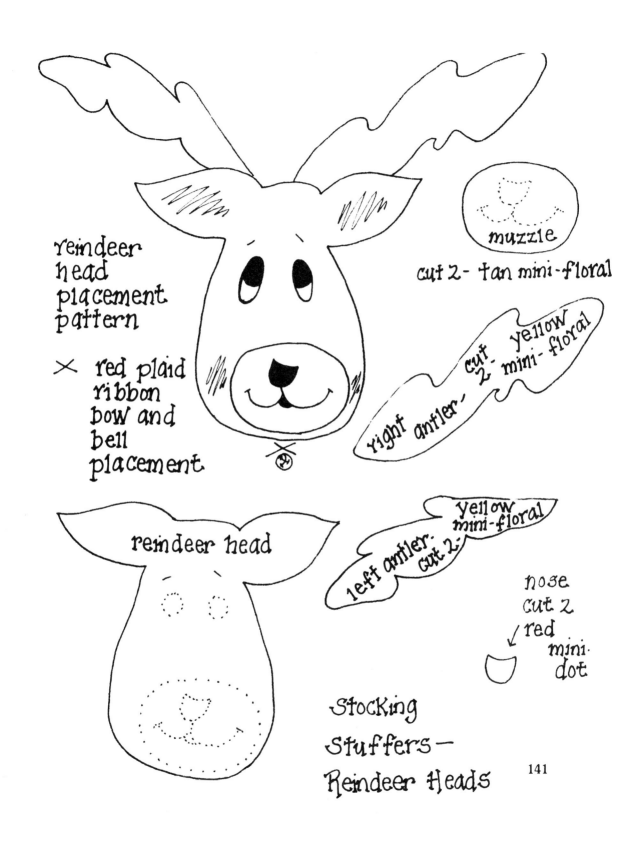

reindeer
head
placement
pattern

✕ red plaid
ribbon
bow and
bell
placement

muzzle

cut 2- tan mini-floral

right antler- cut 2- yellow mini-floral

reindeer head

left antler- cut 2- yellow mini-floral

nose
cut 2
✓red
mini-
dot

Stocking
Stuffers—
Reindeer Heads

141

CHAPTER 6

Professional Pizzazz:
Turning Design into Dollars

After making several projects, and having friends and neighbors admire your talent, thoughts may turn to ways to profit from your new abilities. Start by doing some homework. Study the competition: style, quality, price range. Check with your local government regarding requirements and regulations that affect a home cottage industry. Analyze your costs and time; your price must produce a profit and your labor be cost effective. Store markups are often 50%.

Exhibit your items at a local craft show to see if initial interest is strong. Next, show your clothing and accessories at holiday boutiques or through a Junior League. If you still love every minute of the creating and manufacturing, register your business with your state government for a sales tax number. This is necessary to qualify for trade discounts on large purchases of fabric and trims. Make an appointment with an accountant to set up your business to your best advantage.

I interviewed twelve top boutique owners and buyers for their advice to new cottage industries. Their guidelines will help any new entrepreneur:

1. Use quality materials. If you are marketing your items to sell at $20 wholesale, with a retail price of $40, the quality must warrant the pricing.

2. Workmanship must be professional. Items cannot look homemade. Use buttons and buttonholes, not snaps. Full hems are a must.

3. Quality of samples and quality of delivered merchandise must be comparable. The only business that you will hurt is your own if you deliver items with corners cut or shoddy workmanship.

4. Deliver on time; have invoices and paperwork in order.

If you find that, after analyzing your costs, it is not possible to market your items through a boutique, study alternative marketing ideas. Investigate selling items directly to the public. After checking with local government, consider advertising in the classified section of your newspaper, doing fashion shows in cooperation with local nursery schools, or establishing a home craft party group based on designer clothing for children. Check with charities in the area; you might offer a benefit showing of your clothing, with a percentage of the sales to charity. Check your local library for books on marketing and small business for additional ideas. A beginning list of resources follows to help you launch your business. Good luck!

Sources of
Small Business Information

The Crafts Report
700 Orange St.
Wilmington, DE 19801

Monthly

Craftswoman Magazine
Box 848
Libertyville, IL 60048

Quarterly

Quality Crafts Marketing Magazine
15 W. 44th St.
New York, NY 10036

Quarterly

Sew Business Magazine
1515 Broadway
New York, NY 10036

Monthly

Small Business Administration
1441 L St., NW
Washington, DC 20416

Publishes helpful pamphlets on small business

You may want to check your library for a copy of *Crafts Business Bookshelf, ACC, 1977.* The annotated bibliography will help you find books of interest.

Another helpful resource is *How to Have a Successful Craft Show in Your Home,* by Anne Patterson Dee, available from Daedalus Publications, P.O. Box 848, Libertyville, IL, 60048. A guide to planning and publicizing your own holiday boutique.

Sources of Supplies

General Sewing Supplies

Clotilde
237 SW 28th St.
Ft. Lauderdale, FL 33315

The Fabric Carr
170 State St.
Los Altos, CA 94022

The Felters Co.
22 West St.
Millbury, MA 01527

Acrylic felt

Home-Sew
Bethlehem, PA 18018

Nancy's Notions
PO Box 683
Beaver Dam, WI 53916

Newark Dressmaker Supply
7284 Park Dr.
Bath, PA 18014

The Perfect Notion
115 Maple St.
Toms River, NJ 08753

Susan of Newport
219 20th St.
PO Box 3107
Newport Beach, CA 92663

Stacy Industries, Inc.
38 Passaic St.
P.O. Box 395
Woodridge, NJ 07075

*Thermolam batting and a variety
of interfacings*

Machine-Embroidery Threads

Aardvark Adventures
PO Box 2449
Livermore, CA 94550

Sew-Art International
PO Box 550
Bountiful, UT 84010

SewCraft
Box 6146
South Bend, IN 46660

Speed Stitch
PO Box 3472
Port Charlotte, FL 33952

Treadleart
25834 Narbonne Ave.
Lomita, CA 90717

Embroidery Floss

Craft Gallery
PO Box 8319
Salem, MA 01971

Daisy Chain
PO Box 1258
Parkersburg, WV 26102

Lee Wards
840 N. State St.
Elgin, IL 60120

Children's Patterns

Christmas Everyday
2080 Northridge Dr. NE
Grand Rapids, MI 49505

Folkwear
P.O. Box 3798
San Raphael, CA 94902

Ginger Designs
P.O. Box 3241
Newport Beach, CA 92663

Little Stitches
PO Box 3613
Salem, OR 97302

Muffin & Me
2843 Trenton Way
Ft. Collins, CO 80526

Patch Press
4019 Oakman S.
Salem, OR 97302

Sunrise Designs
PO Box 1316
Orem, UT 84057

Buttons

The Button Shop
PO Box 1065
Oak Park, IL 60304

Factory Outlet Buttons & Things
24 Main St.
Freeport, ME 04032

JHB International, Inc.
1955 S. Quince St.
Denver, CO 80231

Muffin & Me
2843 Trenton Way
Ft. Collins, CO 80526

The Name Game
3324 Gray Moss Rd.
Matthews, NC 28105

Fabrics

Knit Kits
2920 N. 2nd St.
Minneapolis, MN 55411

Lineweaver
3300 Battleground Ave.
Greensboro, NC 27410

Hot Glue Gun

Boycan's Craft
PO Box 897
Sharon, PA 16146

Index

See color insert for all projects.